THE PEOPLE

WIN THROUGH

a play by U NU

with a long biographical introduction by
EDWARD HUNTER

TAPLINGER PUBLISHING CO., INC., NEW YORK 1957

Library of Congress Catalog Card Number: 56–12656

CHARACTERS

U BA THEIN, *retired civil servant*
MA HLA MYINT, *his daughter*
AYE MAUNG, *her suitor*
AUNG WIN, *U Ba Thein's son*
KHIN NWE, *Aung Win's wife*
TET TOE, *their son, ten*
HLA HLA, *their daughter, eight*

White Band Insurgents:
    BOH SAN SHA
    AYE NYEIN
    THA SEIN
    BA TOKE
    BOH MIN YAUNG
    BOH THOUNG HTUT

Villagers:
    Headman of village in Pegu District
    PO SEIK, *schoolmaster*
    PO LIN, *village elder*
    U THA BYAW
    HTWE MAUNG
    Various elders, others

Village Refugee Group:

    MAI SHWE, *country woman*
    U PO MYA, *her husband*
    AYE TIN, *woman*
    DAW PWA, *her mother*
    DAW AYE MAI, *woman*
    U THA DUN
    OHN PE
    MAUNG HTAIK
    U SIN

Army:

    BOH AYE, *platoon commander*
    HLA THOUNG,
    MAUNG LIN,
    PE MYA,
    SEIN MAUNG, *soldiers*

The Communists:

    BOH TAUK TUN, *guerrilla captain*
    CHIT TUN,
    TIN NYUNT,
    SA MI, *guerrillas*
    Other Red guerrilla troops
    Judge in Communist People's Court
    Jury
    Prosecutor
    U SAN KE,
    KO PO LONE,
    THAKIN TUN KHIN,
    BA ZAN, *prisoners*
    U BI, *witness*

THAKIN LUN,
THAKIN SEIN TINT,
THAKIN SAMI, *members Communist Executive
Committee*
Lieutenant, Insurgent group leader

Anti-Communist Guerrilla Group:
    MYA GYI, *leader*
    THA HLA
    Three or four others

Prologue Speaker

INTRODUCTION *by Edward Hunter*

U Nu baffles people who try to label others. He does not fit into any one, neat compartment. Is he a politician or an author? Is he a lawyer or a priest? Is he a radical or a conservative? Is he a Westernized Burmese or a stubborn proponent of old Burmese traditions? Without much difficulty, a good case could be made for any of these labels. Indeed, each is more or less correct. U Nu is a man of tones and blending colors, not of any single, solid hue—white, pink, red, or what you will. This is part of his character.

When Burma won its independence, he became its first Prime Minister. He writes Western-style books, and wears Burmese native attire. He studied law at Rangoon University, and has been a devout Buddhist all of his life. He is a Marxist who has never been a Socialist Party member. He wrote a one-act play in 1934 satirizing the debauchery of Buddhist monks, wrote two domestic satires in 1937, another on Burmese society in 1938, called "Mad Humanity," and a biting drama on the sex life of the middle class Burmese in 1938, called "The Bull at Large." Yet he has been a lifelong crusader for the preservation of the ancient framework of Burmese society.

In Western society, the existence of such diverse traits in the same man would indicate a hopelessly confused individual. But U Nu is not confused. He cannot be explained as if he were a product of London society. His temperament is Burmese. What best describes him is not a professional designation, even of author or politician, but an objective—his country's sovereignty and security. Everything except this objective is subordinate in him. This is why he can be, at the same time, all these different things, yet constitute a harmonious whole, a typical Burmese—perhaps the Burmese who is most typical of this period in his country's history.

I showed his photograph to a mature American who had spent many years in the Orient. After studying the picture for a minute, he hedged by saying, "He's an Asian, and you know how they mask their feelings." This was a superficial impression, but U Nu's wartime career indicates that there is much truth in it; I doubt if the Japanese would deny it. I also showed the photo to a discriminating young art student, who had had no time in which to absorb grown-up patterns of thought, and whose reactions would be unaffected by racial notions. She studied the picture for a minute, and then gave her reaction this way:

"He looks sure of himself. He seems sympathetic and understanding. When he reaches an opinion, I don't think he changes it for anything. He looks cultured and educated."

This was U Nu all right. Professional labels are only a superficial guide to the man; motivation is what counts in him.

In the industrialized West, where specialization has reached exaggerated heights, we have lost some of the wholesome traits of a less modernized society. These are what U Nu has retained. They are what he is aiming at in his neutrality policy. He is trying to be practical and opportunistic, so as to achieve a harmony between his people's languorous past and the requirements of the precise Twentieth Century. He is trying to use the lushness of Burmese nature and character to modify the cold harshness of the industrial age. Such an idyllic formula would be a modern miracle. So the frustrations and the gropings continue in U Nu's lovely land of Burma and in the minds of his volative, simple-hearted people.

U Nu cannot be understood apart from his people; he is intimately related to every phase of their past half-century of humiliation, turmoil, exploitation and bedevilment.

He is a Mongolian-Chinese type, of medium height and width, with a roundish face and small, soft eyes. He has a restful, dreamy look. As he reached maturity he took on the mark of a man of substance, calm, with a well-earned self-assurance.

U Nu was born on May 25, 1907, into a middle-class merchant's family. Hardly a quarter century before, the British had made his country a province of colonial India, removing even the pretense of Burmese autonomy. This was a crude and unstatesmanlike effort to put an end to Burma's recalcitrance. Burmese intractability was not solved by decreeing the merger of the Indian and Burmese territories; the fundamental problem was merely evaded. Burma thus be-

came the colony of a colony. The fallacy that Burma
and India were alike not only allowed their European
masters to exploit Burma, but enabled Burma's big
neighbor to do so, too.

The Burmese generally are dissimilar racially to
the Indians. The latter's aborigines, Negroid and
Australoid, have been pressed south by dark-skinned
Aryan hordes from the northwest, whereas the yellow-
hued Burmese came from Tibet. In India there are
scores of languages, each with numerous dialects, the
most prevalent of these being derived from a Sanskrit
base, with generous borrowings from the Persian and
Arabic. The tonal languages of the Burmese are derived from Eastern sources. Their pronunciation is
akin to the Chinese, although their writing has a
Sanskrit form. The personalities of the Burmese and
the Indians are full of contrasts.

The British, blandly disregarding this conflict in
race, culture and speech — unable even to recognize
these dissimilarities — lumped all these people together as just Asians, and assumed that by the sheer
legalism of a centralized administration, all of these
differences could be made to disappear. This was the
period when the English were evolving a liberal,
laissez-faire doctrine, which relieved their own, chang-
ing society of impossible stresses.

This policy worked well where it evolved naturally
out of Christian culture, with its emphasis on the free
will of the individual. But when imported like a pack-
age of merchandise into a part of the world where it
was neither familiar nor convenient, this noble-sound-
ing, hands-off policy upset such cultural equilibrium as

had already been attained, stymied the natural evolution in beliefs and attitudes, and deprived the weak of such defenses as it had built up. The timing was out of joint, of lop-sided advantage. Instead of spelling out progress, these elements of Western advance meant more stifling evidence of colonialism. Decaying superstitions and dying customs were saved from extinction by the premature enforcement of this doctrine, along with its moral accompaniment of fair play, implemented as if tropical Rangoon was temperate, foggy London. All of this went over the heads of foreign merchant and white crusader alike. They were just not interested; they used these doctrines as a tactic rather than as a principle.

Burma had been relatively independent until the British came in to trade — just trade, as they said. The Burmese saw their country's freedom melt away with this commerce. There was no feudalism in Burma, except among the hill tribes. As social distinctions and class lines develop strongest out of feudal concepts, Burma had little of either. The powerful and rich were few and irresponsible. This gave rise on the other, crowded side of the pendulum to compensating irresponsibility, typified by the peculiar brand of outlaw produced by Burma and India, known as the dacoit.

2

Burma was small and lush, with a rice and bamboo culture freely provided by a bountiful nature. The people lived well, for the soil was magically fertile, except in the cold, rugged hill areas. The country was underpopulated. The people did not have to work hard to make ends pleasantly meet, except during planting and harvest seasons. There was not much to do in the lowlands in the interval, except a little cottage industry, which was not really necessary.

The people lived a lazy, easy life that was reflected in their trustful outlook and their fanciful faith in the spirits of nature — in pixies called nats. They abhorred trade and had no patience for business; they willingly let outsiders attend to such dull matters. The Burmese did not have to buckle down in order to be well fed and comfortably clothed and housed. They did not need the help of others. The people from the hill tribes went into the British army because it gave them a livelihood, and helped support their families. The lowland Burmese had no such incentive, and did not take to army life. They did not like the discipline, and even less did they take to domination. A Burmese, when pressed, would bow to the inevitable, then disappear into the jungle and join the free-wheeling, quick-tempered dacoits. He knew he could never starve in Burma's jungle, which is relatively hospitable to man, in contrast to the Malayan jungle, which cruelly fights the human race. If he had to go into the villages for food and other supplies, these brigands found the peasants not too resentful so long as he grabbed only what little he needed, for everyone knew that there was always more where this come from. This was an idyllic life, but a pushover for speculators and merchants from far and nearby, who came with all the legal appurtenances of Western society.

India was enormous and scorching, where people took to trade with sharp-eyed eagerness. The first effect of the administrative merger and the imported laissez-faire policy was to open the floodgates of Burma to the impoverished Indians, who were being crowded out of their own land by an annual increase in births that alone equaled the entire population of certain European countries. Many came as moneylenders and petty merchants, and between themselves and the competitive Chinese, soon monopolized the business life of Burma. The Indians soon became the biggest landowners in Burma, making the recovery of this good earth, and not domestic land reform, Burma's most critical postwar problem.

The English built up the idea of trade monopoly, and then stood by, guaranteeing peace and order to Indians and Burmese alike, exacting a fee from all indiscriminately, for the multitudinous services they provided.

3

This was U Nu's world. He was a native of Wakema village, in the Myaungmya district, 50 miles west of Rangoon, where the Irrawaddy River splits into half a dozen mouths. His father was a patriotic trader. He sent his son to a government school with misgivings. He admired its high standards in education, and was satisfied that the study of English was obligatory, for he knew how necessary it was for one's future

prosperity. Yet he would have preferred more emphasis on Burmese subjects. He either had to send the lad
to a government school, or forego any pretense of a
modern education for him.

The only other education available was in the
monasteries. This stress on religion came naturally to
the Burmese country boy. Social life in a town or
village was bound by the Buddhist temple, where a
boy normally enrolled for a week or a month as a
novice, just as casually as an American or British
youngster attends a Boy Scout camp. U Nu did so, too,
and like all Burmese youngsters, took lessons in the
sutras and discussed Buddhist teachings with the
monks. He enjoyed excursions to neighboring pagodas.
The Buddhist environment lent itself to an intimacy
between the people and the church. U Nu loved the
color and the glamor of Buddhism.

His Burmese intensity, acquired from his father,
also drew him to Buddhism. He was an intellectual, yet
found in religion a solace that pure intellect could not
provide. His nationalist feelings found an outlet in the
faith of his fathers; nothing else seemed to remain
Burmese any longer. Buddhism had identified itself
with patriotism. Buddhist monks, called pongyis, participated frankly in politics. They were deeply im-
pressed by the work of the Young Men's Christian
Association, brought over from England. The nationalist movement received its flame, as elsewhere in
Asia, from the youth, and the Y. M. C. A. was a youth
movement. This inspired the monks, shortly after
World War I, to organize Young Men's Buddhist Associations. These promptly became an embryo political

party, thus getting around the British ban on political associations. This was the nucleus of Burma's political party system.

The political complexion of the Y. M. B. A. was hardly concealed by the mild-mannered monkhood. One outstanding monk, Sayadaw U Wisara, died a political martyr. Jailed by the British for a seditious speech, he went on a 166-day hunger strike. U Nu must have followed the news about this fasting monk with all the excitement that his American and British cousins displayed for baseball or football. The monk's dying message, "Be wary and wise," might well have been a motto for U Nu.

He was always wary and wise. He led a normal boy's life, although he was scrupulous about rising early enough to have time for prayers in front of his family shrine, before going to school. This gave him a sense of closeness to his own people, that remained with him throughout the day in the foreignized school.

Every schoolboy in the country soon heard the exciting news when the students of Rangoon University went on strike in 1920. They insisted that a new regulation, called the University Act, was discriminatory. Actually, the points raised in the protest were secondary in the minds of the youth. A resentment had been building up for some years over the failure of the British to consult them or any other Burmese when coming to decisions. The actions adopted were secondary in these Burmese minds to the way in which they were reached. The Burmese were weary of being led by others.

A mild sort of united front was already in exist-

ence, in the form of a General Council of Burmese Associations. This was actually an official party, with
village, town and district branches. The student strike
at Rangoon was thus quickly transported, by lay and
clerical channels, throughout the land. This was U
Nu's first political experience, for in his distant village
he, too, went on strike. So did students in government
schools everywhere. As was natural, the boys all re-
paired to their respective pagodas and monasteries,
where they exchanged gossip with the monks, and
eagerly expressed their patriotic feelings.

As the school boycott dragged on, and education
appeared stalemated, older students began to teach
the younger. This year-long walkout was the start of
what became known as national schools, formed by the
Burmese people themselves. These, like government
schools, gave both a primary and secondary education. Although they were not recognized by the government, Burmese opinion was overwhelmingly in
their favor, and U Nu's father gladly transferred his
son to one established in Rangoon. As was to be expected, the curriculum leaned heavily on nationalist
teachings.

A dispute over whether these national schools
should accept government financial aid caused a split
in the General Council of Burmese Associations, and
led to the creation of a group called the People's
Party, which became known to history as the Twenty-
Oners, after the number of its original members. This
group favored the acceptance of such help.

4

U Nu developed normally, entering the college of Rangoon University where he received his bachelor of arts degree, and then went back to his home town, like so many other boys. He settled down contentedly as superintendent of the national school in nearby Pantanaw. Here his duties naturally put him into contact with the president of the school committee, whose daughter caught his eye. She, too, was a devout Buddhist, and the two enjoyed the colorful, timeless environment of pagodas and monasteries. This was 1931. They married, and still make a point of visiting the local Buddhist structures wherever they travel. Her name is Daw Mya Yee — Burmese ladies retain their family name after marriage. Until wedlock, she was "ma," which means female or sister, and then used the prefix "daw," which stands for aunt or elderly, a married woman. She is frequently photographed with her husband, but takes no role in public life. She is the family type. They have five children, aged eight to twenty-one. The eldest and youngest are girls; the other three are boys.

Stirring events were happening on the Asian continent. China was being reunited as a republic under scholarly Dr. Sun Yat-sen and calculating Chiang Kai-shek, and their Kuomintang party was successfully defying the Western Powers. U Nu, along with alert Asians everywhere, was stirred by the Kuomintang's seizure of the British Concession at Hankow and its annulment of many of Britain's economic privileges. These years on the fringe of great events made him restless, and in 1934 he left Pantanaw for good, to study law at Rangoon University.

Japan had already defied the League of Nations, set up the puppet state of Manchukuo, and stage-managed a similar puppet regime in North China. The Pan-Asia movement, under the sponsorship of Nipponese racists, had been developing since the turn of the century. All these created a deep stir among Burmese intellectuals. As an Asian, U Nu sympathized with Japanese rivalry with the West, particularly Britain. The language that was being spoken by distant Moscow, encouraging downtrodden nationalities everywhere, had a great appeal in university circles. From nowhere else were the Burmese receiving even verbal encouragement. Communist propagandists had the field to themselves. This sympathy otherwise would have gone to the United States, because of its revolutionary background and non-colonial record. But only a muted and apologetic voice came from that direction. While the Far East looked toward America, Southeast Asia's attention was on Europe.

Americans were regarded sympathetically, but the Burmese felt that U. S. isolationism was far too deeply ingrained for America to show any effective interest in Burma, and that, anyway, U. S. interests, culturally and racially, were tied in far too much with those of England to be of much use to Burma.

Burmese impressions of the American character and the American way of life were favorable; yet these qualities were negated in the Burmese view by the way Americans fluctuated between sheer materialism and a dangerous naivety. Thus the U. S., that should have become the natural ideal of suppressed peoples everywhere, lost by default.

Burmese independence was the ideal, and socialism was expected to be the means. There was a natural reason for this, for only socialism cleverly identified itself with nationalism, and Marxism seemed synonymous with both. The English residents of Burma, even the poorest, lived in comparative luxury, and most of them occupied pompous homes, in contrast to the residences of the Burmese generally. Socialism promised to put an end to this and all other racial distinctions, and to raise the standard of living. The most quoted lines were not from any poet, but from John Strachey's writing, "from each according to his ability."

The Communist version, "to each according to his needs," did not appeal to U Nu, for he detected the menace in it, although he could hardly yet appreciate the extreme character of the slave philosophy that lurked behind the smooth slogan.

U Nu was a studious young man who walked through the university corridors with his hands clasped behind his back, head bowed in thought. Although pious, he was no prig; in those years he smoked and drank somewhat, giving up both later. He enjoyed the movies, and read a great deal.

He joined the We Burmans Association (Dobama Asiayone), formed a few years previously, and he began to be called Thakin Nu. Thakin meant master, and was used in addressing Englishmen. Burmese men normally were referred to as maung, meaning younger, or ko, the middle-aged, or if very dignified and important, u — just the letter u — meaning uncle, or respected one. Until then U Nu had usually been addressed as Maung Nu — even today he modestly signs him name Maung Nu, although he is addressed with the more lofty title.

The Dobama youth asked why the Burmese word thakin should only refer to foreigners. Were Burmese not the equal of aliens? They determined to use this prefix in addressing Burmese, too. One Dobama member wrote what rapidly became Burma's national song. Its passionate tunes had much to do with U Nu, and others who are now national heroes, joining the organization. The members were mostly intellectuals, who laid great stress on reading foreign radical literature, much of which was Soviet.

U Nu became active in university affairs, joining the Student Union and writing for student publications. A circle formed of friends who were to leave their mark on Burmese history. If anyone had predicted that within fifteen years, the assassination of one of these young men would elevate U Nu to the Premiership of an independent Burma, he would have been considered mad.

U Nu became president of the Student Union in 1936, when dissatisfaction was coming to a head in the university. Burmese were becoming increasingly indignant over the second-rate jobs they were limited to in their own country.

The principal, an English educator, had no patience for these youthful Burmese resentments. The university, reflecting the pettifogging policies of government, proceeded as if nothing ever changed in the world. Anglo-Indians seemed to be the new privileged class, and the better jobs went to them, rather than even to Anglo-Burmese.

One of U Nu's characteristics was to sit quietly in a meeting, listening to what others had to say, until finally, as if his thoughts had assembled doggedly within him, he would rise and let flow his pent-up ideas. Something like this must have been responsible for his daring speech to the Student Union one day on the need for a drastic overhauling of the university faculty. He was promptly called on the carpet by the principal, who ordered him to apologize, meanwhile suspending him from classes.

A youth named Aung San was editor of the university's student paper, called "Orway," which means "Voice of the Peacock," the proud, richly plumed bird that is Burma's significant national emblem. "Orway" appeared with a biting criticism of a professor, and Aung San was called on the carpet, too, and ordered to apologize, and to tell who had written the article. He refused, and the unimaginative dean could think of nothing more salutary than his expulsion.

These incidents sparked an immediate strike by the irritated student body. U Nu found himself overnight the leader of a nationwide student's walkout. All government and national schools throughout the land joined up at once.

5

A headquarters was promptly set up in a resthouse on a hillside road adjoining Burma's great Schwedagon Pagoda, the most venerated Buddhist

temple in the Indo-Chinese countries. The selection of
this spot for a strike headquarters was nothing casual;
the Burmese mind turned this way in times of crisis.
This identification with the cultural patterns of the
past made the radical departures of the present appear
less strange and forbidding, and gave great strength.

U Nu had an instinct for gaining such spiritual
support. Frequently, during the strike, he would retire to the calm of one of the numerous prayer halls
on the enormous temple grounds, to meditate and ar-
range his thoughts, and gain confidence-giving peace
of mind in the midst of a struggle in which the odds
were all weighted on the opposing side. Messengers
were frequently sent into the pagoda from strike headquarters to inform him of some late development, and
to receive instructions. He felt capable of more astute
judgment in this timeless environment.

He gave numerous speeches. His words, a trifle
shrill, somewhat emotional, were clear and forceful
— he was an effective orator. Usually modest, convey-
ing an impression of deep sincerity, he won sympathetic
attention. In those days he wore no glasses — he now
wears reading glasses.

The strike ended inconclusively after dragging
on for four months, giving U Nu his first practical
training in politics, and earning him nationwide recognition as a pioneer "rebel leader." He was now
also being referred to by a nickname, "The Bull Let
Loose," or Natho Kyopyat, a coloquialism indicating
a man who will go to any extent to accomplish his goal.

6

The students resumed their classes, but U Nu had found new interests. He had done a great deal of writing during the strike, and now wanted to concentrate on a literary career. He founded a leftwing book club called the Red Dragon (Nagani), that attempted to encourage a modern Burmese literature along Marxian and Shavian lines, and which translated representative Western books. His eclectic character showed up in his choice of the first book that he translated, Dale Carnegie's "How to Win Friends and Influence People." Everything he wrote had significance, usually political, in the Shavian manner of the day.

Before Burma could free itself from England, it first had to divorce itself from India. This marriage at pistol point had become a heated domestic issue. Some important London circles realized by now how unfair this was, and were seeking an annulment. As soon as some nationalist circles in Burma heard that London was showing a more tolerant attitude regarding this unnatural marriage of the two countries, they came out in its defence. Anti-British feeling had become so dogmatic that no matter how commendable, any policy or action could be almost irreconcilably smeared by receiving British support. So much of what London had presented to the Burmese as above-board, generous treatment had turned out the opposite in effect that they now distrusted anything that emanated from Albion.

In 1937, Burma's galling status of a province

was ended by a plebiscite that made it merely a British colony. The British governor of Burma took over the prerogatives of the Viceroy of India, while both were subordinated to a Secretary of State for India and Burma in London, who was separate from the Colonial Office.

Lack of responsibility remained the crippling characteristic of the Burmese legislature, already in existence since 1920. A dozen Burmese splinter political parties operated like debating clubs. If determination to rule themselves were the criterion, Burma was on the rapid road to sovereignty, yet the moderating and educational effects of responsibility were lacking. Under normal circumstances, these could be slowly learned by trial and error; only the time was not normal — the world outside was in too much turmoil to let Burma work out her destiny in peace. Burma's numerous leaders, mostly in their twenties — a political leader in his thirties was well advanced in years —violently opposed each other on almost every issue except one, their ultimate objective. They all wanted Burma to become wholly free. Opinions on how to achieve this ranged from one stratagem to another. Everyone admitted that without allies, Burma could never force the British to disgorge it.

Without allies, the only alternative was to take advantage of England's difficulties. This was a policy of sheer desperation, by a weak, broken country, in existence hardly a thousand years. This was why the idealistic youth of Burma, in one of the numerous anamolies of the age, looked hopefully toward the rising star of the least idealistic of all men on earth —

Hitler — as their own hope for the future. They really did not want Hitler and his Nazism to achieve world supremacy; what they hoped was that Hitler would become strong enough to crack England, so as to force it to give Burma its freedom. Their hope was that somehow, then, as the wheel of fortune turned, the Nazis would be incapable of expanding into Asia, and that Burma would remain free. This was the constantly recurring motive, that obscured every other consideration.

Burmese policy boiled down to a maneuvering to take advantage of British difficulties with Germany.

The young Burmese intellectuals listened with bewildered fascination to the chest-pounding of German nazis, Japanese ultranationalists and Italian fascists. The shrill, little answering cry made by England, which roared like a lion when dealing with the Burmese, gave them pause — and pleasure. The earnest logic of the Western democracies sounded appealing enough, but the weak example they set belied their words, and strengthened the ages-old habit of the Asians to appraise every situation inside a power framework. After uttering kindly sentiments and persuasive words, the Westerners themselves relapsed back into a power framework. The Burmese could not make head nor tail out of this frenetic exchange of charge and countercharge. Only so far as all this ranting gave them the opportunity to advance their own nationalist ends did they see any sense in it. Sincere, sacrificial purpose, and calculated, sheer opportunism, looked superficially alike.

Nonetheless, Burmese intellectuals were inclined

toward democratic concepts; they distrusted dictatorship, for they had undergone too much of it themselves. Yet, each time the British, French or Dutch, came out with what sounded like conclusive arguments, they could not rid their minds of personal experiences, when similarly enticing phrases, once agreed to, had become a medium for harsh, humiliating, exploitative pressures.

How could they believe those people now? This was the tragedy of the West's relations with the East. All that the Burmese could be sure of was the success of the Nazis, Fascists and fanaticized Shintoists. Anyone who opened his eyes and ears could not avoid seeing who was making headway. About the only philosophy they could apply to their own lives was contained in the writings of such diverse, materialistic characters as Karl Marx, Upton Sinclair and Dale Carnegie. If there were great gulfs between them, they seemed incidental.

7

So it was that when Japanese agents, fresh from victory in Manchuria, North China and Indo-China, came to Burma with high-sounding promises, they were listened to respectfully, and their offers accepted. They promised, without any hemming or hawing, that Burma would be completely free. The British refused even to consider such a pledge. Whether the Japanese meant what they promised was beside the point so far as the Burmese were concerned. The facade was better than nothing. Who could tell, once the facade had been built, the opportunity might come to erect the rest of the structure? Buddhism teaches that the wheel always turns; one need only be patient.

Britain was fighting valiantly, in the Col. Blimp manner, for its survival in Europe. Yet, so far as U Nu and his Burmese comrades could detect, the attitude of the British colonial administrators in Burma had undergone no change. They casually assumed that Rangoon would unquestioningly follow the British lead in the war. If this were a war against aggression, for the survival of free people, the Burmese intellectuals declared that they of course were on London's side, providing that England backed up its words by the specific promise that Burma could be free, once the war had been won. This seemed to them a fair test of British sincerity.

Burma had already won many of the appurtenances of a self-governing dominion, but these no longer satisfied. This was the climax of the dismal war period characterized on the Allied side by the catch phrase, too little and too late. The Burmese Legislature was headed by U Saw, a radical leader of little education but plenty of native shrewdness. He came from the Tharrawaddy region, fifty miles to the north of Rangoon, where the last rebellion against the British had erupted in 1950, when infuriated Burmese clashed madly with the Indian community. This area, and Shwebo, were considered the cradle of Burmese nationalism, constituting the Wild West of Burma, where disrespect for law was as proverbial as in the vigilante days of California.

U Saw was Minister of Education at the time of the Rangoon University strike. He was jealous of the Premier, an eloquent intellectual named Dr. Ba Maw, and used every parliamentary wile to weaken him. U Saw organized a number of splinter parties into a coalition. He unseated Ba Maw and became Premier himself by cleverly exploiting dissatisfaction over the outcome of the strike, and the failure of the government to implement the impossible Socialist pledges it had so glibly promised.

U Saw introduced a number of much needed reforms, easing land tenure and tenancy requirements, and providing some measure of farm relief. Then he went to London, to negotiate with Winston Churchill, who now headed the British war government. U Saw insisted on an absolutely ironclad promise of postwar freedom, with no ties of any sort with London. Churchill would have none of it. He had U Saw arrested in January, 1942, for being in contact with the Japanese enemy. He was taken from London to the British African protectorate of Uganda, where he was held throughout the war.

Dr. Ba Maw had as few scruples as U Saw, but greater talent. Back in 1931, he had helped organize the Anti-Separation League against Burma's release from Indian administration, when the British seemed ready to grant it. He became the predominant figure in Burmese politics when civilians joined the Buddhist priests who were pioneering in pro-nationalist activities.

Ba Maw's wife, daughter of a wealthy Mandalay diamond merchant, had boundless faith in his political possibilities. He was an ordinary student with little money when she married him. She financed his entry into politics with her family jewels. He espoused socialism, calling his version the sinyetha (proletarian) policy. The simple formula of making everyone an equal owner of Burma's vast resources and potentially enormous productivity appealed strongly to the plain people and the intellectuals alike.

B Maw, who believed that any means justified the end, preferred extremist shortcuts. With U Saw out of the way, he called a meeting of the splinter groups, including U Nu's and gave them a fiery talk, demanding independence as the price for Burmese wartime support of Britain. This made it unanimous. In Axis emulation, he was elected dictator of this coalition, which thereupon went underground, calling itself the Burma Freedom League.

The Japanese promise to help the Burmese expel the British and to set up their own government looked more inviting than ever to the young Burmese. The situation had so deteriorated that there was no clear demarcation line between a sincere Burmese nationalist and a Burmese who lent himself to Japanese machinations for personal advantage. The British response was to arrest all the young Burmese leaders they could find. Thirty managed to escape, and were next heard of in Japan, which gave them a haven, military training and political indoctrination. The British located U Nu and Ba Maw, and clapped them into prison. For all their nearsightedness and stupidity, the British clung to the basic principles that marked their way of life; if it had been the Axis whom they had crossed, these Burmese patriots would have been summarily executed.

As the Japanese invaders pressed forward, the British shifted the imprisoned Burmese leaders from one jail to another. Just before the Japanese seized Mandalay, the British found that holding U Nu was too much of a burden, and released him. At the time this appeared to be more evidence of British hesitancy and weakness. In the long run it paid off. In the free Burma of today, a freedom which the circumstances of the mid-twentieth Century made inevitable, the Premier became this same U Nu — and he has a fine memory.

Incarceration provided U Nu with the material for a novel on prison life called "Oh, How Cruel!" which he completed in 1940 after he was freed. The book, which contains a goodly share of lurid romance, became quite popular during the Japanese occupation.

Japanese agents, appreciating the hold that Buddhism had on the country, exerted much of their influence on Buddhist monks. They used any tactic that would work, from specious promises to flattery and corruption. As a consequence of this positive effort, while the British upheld merely the negative, the Japanese Armies won the decisive, fifth column assistance of the monks. The allied front crumpled in front of this seepage.

Ba Maw's wife was not going to be cheated of fame by anything so prosaic in Burmese history as an invasion from abroad. She contacted the Japanese, strings were pulled, and her husband was released from prison. A few days later the Japanese Army set him up as their puppet premier. Ba Maw defended his actions to me after the war this way:

"We Burmese had no alternative but to follow expediency rather than a policy. I spent most of my life following expedients instead of a policy. I had to fool people, to lie and to fight. Remember that a desperate people, trying to find a way out, will take any recourse that is offered. I would take any way out, and damn the consequences."

8

When the Japanese succeeded in overrunning Burma, after coming all the thousands of miles through China, Indo-China and Thailand (Siam), the Burmese could see no prospect of their losing the war. The British had just given a demonstration of lack of purpose and retreat that was unbelievable a few months before. If Burma were ever to achieve freedom, it seemed to the young, bewildered and thoroughly excited Burmese leaders that this could only come through arrangement with the Berlin-Tokyo setup.

U Nu joined Ba Maw's government, their parties merging under the combined name of Dobama Sinyetha, with U Nu as secretary general. The thirty Burmese who had taken refuge in Japan returned to Burma widely publicized as the "Thirty Heroes," leading a so-called Burmese Independence Army, headed by none other than U Nu's college editor, Aung San. This brigade came in with the Japanese Army, along the bloody and cruel Moulmein route to Rangoon. Many a stray

Britisher who gave himself up or was trapped by the brigade was summarily shot at pistol point. Their lives paid for resentments built up over a period of one hundred and fifty years.

Aung San's brigade was the nucleus of what Tokyo expected would become a puppet army that could take its place alongside similar puppet military forces being recruited among the Chinese and the Indians. Except for propaganda effect, none of these artificially-created armies repaid the efforts expended on them.

If inflammatory speeches and demonstrative troop reviews could have won battles, the Burmese aid to the Japanese would have soundly thrashed the allies. U Nu, first as Foreign Minister and later as Minister for Publicity and Propaganda, played his role eloquently.

Burma was declared independent by the Japanese on August 1, 1943, in ceremonies that were staged like a play. Aung San's army was reorganized as the Burma Defense Army, and he was alloted the post of Minister of Defense. His troops accepted training and supplies with enthusiasm, but neither the coaxings nor the roars of the frustrated Japanese sergeants and generals could induce them to actually go out and fight.

Whenever the Japanese pressed for action the Burma Defense Army discovered the lack of some critical equipment that first had to be supplied — by the Japanese, of course. Or existing equipment required urgent repairs, that had to be made by the Japanese, too. Or more intensive training was required, or the transportation system was inadequate. Any one of a multitude of excuses for inaction were always at hand. The Japanese had more than suspicion, they knew that they were being given the runaround. But they had erected this Burmese facade of independence, and could not stop the show without ripping a glaring hole, visible to all other Asians, in their much-touted All-Asia Co-Prosperity Sphere.

Some Burmese acted as if this were no show, but the real thing. This fluctuation between play-acting and the genuine even confused the Japanese. They took recourse in a waiting game, but this time they were not dealing with the impatient West, but with fellow Asians who could wait more patiently than they.

As the months rolled by, the Burmese began to detect two fallacies in their line of reasoning. They noted that the Co-Prosperity Sphere, which the Japanese totalitarians had made the cornerstone of their war policy, was completely one-sided. The Japanese gave every indication that Burmese freedom was to be in name alone; in all else the Japanese militarists ruled with an iron fist that thrust metallic fingers into every phase of Burmese life, from the religious to the economic. Under the cloak of guidance and cooperation, the Burmese noticed that even their industry and resources were being transferred to Japanese ownership.

The Burmese began to note, too, that the Japanese Army, for all its claim to a divine, anthropomorphic link to the gods, was no more invincible than any other human beings. This army had plunged ahead into a sensational invasion of India, and then was seen being thrust back after penetrating only a few miles. Soon Japan's best divisions were seen beginning to be slowly but surely ground to pieces. Reinforcements of Japan's best troops from the Kwantung Peninsula in Manchuria merely added grist to the mill. None of this could be concealed from the people on the spot.

Once there was evidence that the Japanese Army was not unconquerable, the Burmese reacted accordingly, their sights still fixed on their sole objective, their country's freedom.

Toward the end of March, 1945, all possible preparations were completed, all possibly needed supplies were on hand, and all the training that could be required had been given to the Burmese Defense Army. The time for hedging was over; the announcement was made with great fanfare that it was going out to fight the enemy. The Burmese troops were ceremoniously cheered as they marched from their barracks. Busy Japanese newspaper photographers, always a barometer of Tokyo's concern, ran back and forth, and climbed up and down. Scores of photos were snapped, but none were ever published, for this was the last the Japanese saw of Aung San. The next the Japanese heard was that Burmese soldiers were attacking their garrison in Pegu. Then the Burma Defence Army seemed to melt away. When Japanese military police began rounding up young pedestrians on the Rangoon streets in a search for arms, it was evident to the people that Aung San and his men had gone underground.

U Nu must have maintained his ties with Aung San all along. A number of the Burmese government heads, while operating openly as Japanese puppets, must have simultaneously winked upon, and wherever possible facilitated, clandestine underground operations against the Japanese. As the balance of power slowly shifted in the Pacific war, so did the Rangoon regime. Without such backing in high places, Aung San could never have perpetrated his daring exploits.

Germany was tottering, and its surrender was only a short way off. The Burmese realized that there was little likelihood of Japan alone withstanding the combined power of the Allies. As the Japanese retreated, and the Allies landed, U Nu left the government. He immediately joined the underground, as its Vice President.

The hill people to the north, adhering to their sectional differences, and closely tied to the Americans by religious ties, especially Baptist, helped the Allies sacrificially and with extraordinary bravery from the very start. Their tribal cohersion had not yet been weakened by nationalism, and so the Marxian ideology could make no imprint on them. Without the help given by the Kachins and the Chins, Gen. Joseph W. Stilwell could never have returned to Burma, or laid the Burma pipeline. The separatist tendencies of these tribes after the war became, next to the Communists, the biggest headache of the Rangoon government. Their feeling of being let down by those whom they had formerly helped courageously was to enable the Reds to make serious inroads among them. This presented the reborn Burmese nation with a gruelling test of its tolerance and statesmanship.

When the war ended, U Nu said he was returning

to his first love, writing, and would leave politics behind him. The English brought back the colonial government that had fled to Simla, the luscious summer
capital of the Indian colonial administrators, located
on the ridge of the Himalayas almost out of this world.
Equipped with reams of projects written in gobblygook,
these administrators, who had fled precipitously, now
stepped out of these clouds, back into Burma. The same
faces showed up, with the same titles, as if the war
years had not intervened.

They came with no noticeable change in attitude
toward the Burmese people. They brought a political
offer of Dominion status, with equal rights in the British Commonwealth. This would have been considered
generous some years back, but already, on the eve of
the Japanese invasion, had been too little and too late.

9

The underground had united all Burmese elements
into an Anti-Fascist People's Freedom League
(AFPFL), under the leadership of Aung San. He
bluntly refused to participate in an Executive Council
with only advisory powers, as was set up by the returning Governor, Sir Reginald Dorman-Smith.

The Communists, as part of the Freedom League,
gave an ominous warning of what was to come by
making extravagant claims to having taken the ma-
jor, if not the exclusive role, in the wartime underground. Quiescent for the most part during the war,
now that propaganda channels were again available,

they went speedily into high gear to create the impression that they had been leading the opposition and doing all the fighting. The secrecy under which the underground had had to operate enabled the Reds to lay claim to every exploit that was not nailed down in public knowledge.

The situation was fast getting nowhere, and nerves were being skinned raw once again by indecision and double-talk, when the new Labor Party government in England made up its mind; it decided to let the Burmese have their own way at once, and sent out a soldier, Maj. Gen. Sir Hubert Rance, to become governor. He admired Aung San, and promptly invited him to form the Executive Council, in Cabinet fashion. Thus a stop-gap rule, by Burmese who had the people's backing, was improvised until a final settlement could be made. This arrangement, without political subterfuge and diplomatic evasion, cut the gordian knot and opened the way to an harmonious outcome of the 200-year Anglo-Burmese relationship. Prime Minister Attlee announced, just before Christmas of 1946, that a Burmese delegation was to be invited to London to determine details of transfer of power to Burma.

Aung San, as chief of the National Front, naturally led it, arriving in London on January 9, 1947, with leaders of the various political elements, including U Saw, whom the British had released at the war's end, as they had promised. He immediately resumed his all-or-nothing, rule-or-ruin tactics. U Nu stayed in Burma, in a position to handle whatever problems might arise in case of any untoward development. As

Aung San said on the eve of his departure, "I hope for the best, but I am prepared for the worst." People already looked up to U Nu after Aung San.

Aung San, as chief of the wartime underground, was affectionately regarded by the whole Burmese public. He was not an easy man to work with, and violated the traditional behavior patterns of his people in order to get things done. In a part of the world where initiative and the ability to come to a decision with clarity and effectiveness had been suppressed, he had the capacity to make up his own mind quickly and decisively.

The outcome of the London conference was a settlement as generous as that made by the United States with the Philippines. The Aung San-Attlee Agreement, dated January 27, 1947, allowed Burma to determine whether it wished to remain in or out of the British Commonwealth, and provided for a peaceful, peacetime transfer of sovereignty to the Burmese people — not with loopholes, but intact.

The only dissenting voices were raised by Thakin Ba Sein, president of Dobama Asiayone, and U Saw. Nothing less than utter, immediate relinquishment of all ties, as if England had never existed, as if the Burmese people had always been fully free and experienced, was acceptable to them. If both the Burmese and the English had been able to look into the future only a few years, they would have understood the grim warning implied in a remark U Saw had made in a speech for his own Myochit (Patriot) Party only a while back. If London did not accede to

Burmese demands, Burma would be fully justified in seeking help from other foreign quarters, he had declared. The only other "foreign help" could have been from Soviet Russia. That he could have made such a blatant statement without some understanding having been reached through clandestine Communist channels was doubtful. U Saw filled the qualifications that Moscow has always found most useful in a foreign front.

U Saw said he saw in the provisions of the Aung San-Attlee agreement a vehicle for continued British domination over Burma. That he was indulging only in obstructionist tactics was evident from the generous wording of the pact. Only a short while was to pass before U Saw himself was to provide incontrovertible evidence that personal jealousy of Aung San, who had named him to the delegation, had become an obsession with him. His intransigeance permitted no recognition of good-will on an opposing side, and would accept nothing less than total acquiescence to his will.

The British government bowed to Aung San's demand for full freedom, requiring only that details be worked out by an elected Constituent Assembly that would draft a Constitution. Aung San had made this demand on behalf of the Freedom League even before V-J Day, immediately after the start of the Allied liberation of Burma from Japanese occupation.

When the mission returned home, U Nu returned once more to his writing. This time it was to be a permanent divorce from politics. His country's independence assured, he felt he could now become a private citizen. He did not even run in the general elections for a Constituent Assembly.

But destiny did not allow him to retire. An elected member was drowned in a coastal wreck, and pressure was put on U Nu to fill the vacated post. He entered an uncontested by-election, and so became part of the Assembly, alongside the numerous resistance leaders. He was promptly elected speaker. The Assembly convened on June 10, 1947, and the next day unanimously approved an independence resolution that already had been passed upon by a convention of the Freedom League, that was virtually a rehearsal for the forthcoming Assembly, with mostly the same delegates, and Aung San presiding.

Now that the unity movement was approaching an unexpectedly fast success, the Communists began to show their teeth, breaking into Stalinist and Trotskyist factions, snarling at each other and at the nascent government. U Nu, dedicated to a free Burma, to whom all the vacillations, machinations and intrigues that had been engaged in during the war could only be justified by a nationalist, patriotic motivation, was shocked and repelled by this evidence that there were some for whom Burma's independence drive was only a means to a wholly different end. Wartime unity constituted only a tactic and not a policy for these Burmese, who now acted as if they were foreign imperialists.

The political climate was brightening fast, and U Nu himself now headed a Burmese Goodwill Delegation to London, that paid tribute to those who had

fallen in the liberation war, and at the same time
settled additional details in the Aung San-Attlee Agreement.

The Constitution was slowly taking final form
in the Assembly. Some startling rumors began to be
heard that an attempt was going to be made on the
life of Aung San. These were too fantastic to be believed. Rumors had all along been one of the chief
propaganda weapons in the late war, and everyone
was inured to them by now. The more elaborate they
were, the more quickly they were discounted. So nobody paid any heed to these, particularly as it seemed
so completely improbable that so beloved a leader as
Aung San could be the target of a plot at this late
date, on the eve of Burma's rebirth as a sovereign state.

10

Aung San summoned a Cabinet meeting for July
19. This promised to be another routine session, for
the impetuous young men of Burma now were confident that they had history under control. Only the
details remained to be implemented. That Aung San,
who had led such a crowded life, was only 32 years of
age, was not surprising in the new Burma, but was
indicative of the pace at which its youth had lived.
History had to run to keep pace with them. U Nu was
an elder in this company; he was a round forty.

Ten ministers and two secretaries filed into the
Council chamber of the massive Secretariat buildings
that tragic morning. U Saw was not among them; he

was outside the government, stubbornly opposed to
the whole procedure, unless he could have everything
his own way, and under his control. He was becoming
more and more desperate as Burma's emancipation
approached. In his blurred vision, he saw only Aung
San and the others dominating him. Before the prospect of someone else's obtaining the laurels he felt
should fit around his own brow, he lost his thin coat-
ing of parliamentary trappings, and relapsed back into
a dacoit mentality.

Only the extremists, the Communists, favored him
now. They flattered him. An attempt was made to as-
sassinate him, and this aggravated his fixation. He
added two and two, and came up with twenty-two.
Aung San personified in his heated brow all his difficulties.

He convinced himself that the Aung San-Attlee
Agreement was only a new form of bondage, and
that the British could not — must not — be trusted.
He became obsessed with the conviction that there had
to be some trick in it, and that he had been selected by
destiny to prevent it. Marx and Lenin had taught him
that the capitalist countries would never relax their
stronghold on a colonial land or on a proletarian people except by force and violence. This was dogma, and
so his own, fanaticized mind insisted that it be accepted, unquestioned.

At 10:30 a.m. that mad morning, the door to the
Council chamber opened and a small band of men
walked in. Aung San must have thought it curious
that they had not been announced; maybe his instinct
told him what was being attempted, but if so, there

was no time for the unarmed Cabinet members to do anything about it, for the intruders at once began spraying the room with bullets.

The rat-tat-tatting, ricocheting shots immediately killed Aung San, his younger brother, U Ba Win, an unostentious Mandalay school-master; Mahn Ba Khaing, a Karen noted for his silvery-tongued command of the Burmese language; Mongpawn Saopha — ruling chief of Mongpawn — who brought modernization into agriculture; Thakin Mya, one of the original thakins, a hard-working nationalist politician, Deedoke U Ba Choe, outstanding journalist, an authority on Burmese literature and art; and a secretary. The rain of bullets also fatally wounded Sayagyi Abdul Razak, a titled Moslem whose nationalist fervor had made him popular. He died in a hospital the next day. An Education Ministry functionary who rushed to the doorway was slain as the killers dashed out.

One of the assassins was reported to have then gone to the Legislature to hunt for U Nu, who belonged to the inner circle, although he was not a member of the Cabinet. Fortunately he was not there at the time.

Never in Parliamentary history had there been such a coup. This was a carry-over from the past, irresponsible epochs of personal rule, of a despotism that changed hands only by personal intrigue and merciless, personal jealousies of no concern to the people, except as they would have to suffer and die on behalf of some purposeless chief. This was the way blind dogma logically expressed itself.

The saddest aspect of the mass killing was that

it was so utterly bereft of meaning. The killers, rounded up by evening, had been actuated wholly by personal jealousy. They wanted power. They were incapable of submitting to parliamentary limitations. The demand that almost overnight, such democratic processes be observed without an intervening, deep spiritual struggle was to require the impossible. A child does not grow up overnight — except through a soul-rearing tragedy that either deforms it permanently, or gives it great dignity and wisdom. Which would it be for Burma?

Some of this must have sunk into the Burmese soul that day, for its response was not mob vengeance, for which there was certainly extreme provocation, but orderly processes of law. Thousands peacefully lined the streets outside Jubilee Hall, where the bodies of the slain were laid out.

U Saw was the leader of the murder gang. He and six confederates were ultimately executed, and death sentences were passed on two others. A ninth was given life imprisonment for turning informer. Others must have been involved whose names never came out, for this was a large group in the know.

U Nu would surely have been a Cabinet member, and so also would likely have been among the slain, if he had not been the assembly speaker. To this he owed his life. The assassins' bullets brought his country to the crossroads between advancing as a sovereign nation, or relapsing back, like U Saw, into tribal hates and vengeances. At such a decisive moment, the paramount need was for a non-controversial figure, who had the faculty of bringing people together, who was

not an antagonistic element, but who had a calming
influence on people and factions alike, able to con-
ciliate opposing groups. U Nu, as Vice President of
the Freedom League as well as Assembly head, was the
rightful successor to Aung San. On his shoulders was
slipped the mantle of power that had fallen from the
stricken hero's body.

Throughout, as always in his career, U Nu remained the passive type, patiently counting his Buddhist beads. His confidence in destiny brought him close
to his people. Their gambling trait, against which
U Nu often inveighed, was the crude form of his
fatalistic approach.

Life had surely contributed its utmost to support
U Nu's confidence in destiny. Three times now, at the
most epochal moments of his life, destiny had decided
for him, making happen what had seemed highly improbable, if not impossible. The first time was when
the British released him from prison, whereas they
might just as well have held him abroad during the
war, as they did U Saw. He could easily have been
held at least in India. Instead, he was let loose, and Ba
Maw chose him for a key Cabinet post.

The second time, a shipwreck, with the resultant
death of an Assembly member, brought him back into
the forefront of public life. The third time, almost an
entire Cabinet was wiped out to make way for him.

As if this were a debt owed to Aung San, the
Assembly worked fast and harmoniously on the Constitution. When the draft was completed, U Nu took
it to London. Contrary to what the British fervently
hoped, and what had taken place in India, where

Dominion ties were knotted, little Burma decided to go it all alone. London accepted the Burmese decision with the traditional sportsman's smile and handshake. London affixed its signature to a treaty by which Burma stepped outside of the British Commonwealth, while retaining friendly ties. Arrangements were concluded for a British military mission to be set up in Burma for instructional purposes alone. This continued only until late 1953.

The Declaration of Independence was announced in the 1,109th year of Burmese history, on January 4, 1948. The declaration included this pledge to the world:

> *As a free people, we shall discharge the duties that the free peoples of the world's free nations discharge.*

In similar vein, the document concluded:

> *Just as we love and value our freedom, we shall love and value the freedom of other sister nations of the world family; and just as we hold peace and security dear to our hearts, we shall contribute to the protection of world peace and security together, joining hands with the other peoples who also hold peace and security as dear as we do.*

The Socialist Party was the largest in the Freedom League, so when the first, national elections in 1951 swept the League into power, this Marxist organization won overwhelming control of the government. U Nu was voted back into office by a Rangoon constituency. As the top man of the Freedom League, although not a Socialist Party member, Parliament elected U Nu as Premier.

Far from this bringing the story to an end, it was just the preface for U Nu and his country. Now they could no longer escape from the inflexible demands of ultimate responsibility. If they failed, what would be lost would be their own and their country's freedoms.

11

The Marxist leanings of the men in power made it painful and difficult for them to recognize and adopt adequate measures against the treason of others who, while Communists, called themselves Marxist, too. They had all grown up and suffered together. All through life, these young Burmese had had to learn the hard way, by trial and error, by torture and death. Now they were to be taught the true nature of Communism, also the hard way. U Nu's conciliatory nature was more and more tried.

He attempted to be realistic by leading Burma to the head of the list of countries, outside the Soviet bloc, that recognized the Communist Chinese regime which was set up at Peking on October 1, 1949. The reality of the long, common border between the Chinese mainland and northern Burma, a frontier that was still controversial at some points, made this seem practical to U Nu. Anyway, London was recognizing Red China, too, and using its influence to persuade others to do so, in accordance with a pledge arrogantly insisted on by Peking. Yet nothing less than complete subserviance was acceptable to the Communist Party, with the same intransigeance that had motivated U Saw.

The insurgent leaders had been able to work together when the primary objective of each was the same, the attainment of Burmese sovereignty. Now that this was accomplished, they were confronted with the requirements of an entirely different and more complicated way of life. Many of them had never known a day without recrimination of England. The English had submitted. What were they to do now?

The Communists insisted that England had all along been identified with imperialism, and that imperialism was still the enemy. Aung San had seen the danger to his country's hard-won freedom in this specious argument. In a speech in mid-1947 before the preindependence Rehabilitation Conference, he had boldly adjusted himself to new conditions, declaring:

> *We will be only wasting our time and energy by attacking imperialism at this stage. In the past it was the fashion for many of us to blame imperialism for every ill in the country. Speaking for myself, I believe that this was substantially true at one time. No country could really prosper, no people could be self-sufficient, under the imperialistic sway of any other country. But things have changed in this country since.*

The common, independence platform had now lost its main plank. What remained were a vague Marxian faith and a doctrinaire socialism unchanged from before the war. Each insurgent leader brought over new planks that he was positive would support the traffic of post-war security. Each leader was positive that he was as brave and capable as the next, and each, too, was confident that his planks were the sturdiest. Until U Nu's Freedom League won the actual election, nobody could argue with any of these that he did not represent the popular will.

Nationalism was the dominant factor, yet it had not yet progressed to a coherent understanding of national adhesion and a long-range view of national security. The development of a democratic attitude of give and take was the responsibility of U Nu's government. If democracy was enforced from the top down, the example set for the people could very well contradict democracy. Could the government institute a self-educationary process, that would rise from the bottom up, out of the will and by the growing experience of the people?

Marxism, with its stress on centralized controls, motivated against this. So did the foreign aid programs, that operated between governments solely. Under such circumstances, the only alternative left for the Burmese government was to learn by trial and error and by experience, just as the people. This would be the historic test of the sincerity of the new regime. Fortunately for Burma, the man at the helm was the spiritual, essentially non-doctrinaire U Nu.

With Aung San's assassination, there remained few if any Burmese leaders who had his capacity for reaching a timely and clear decision, and clinging tightly to it, irrespective of the traditional "channel of influence" system, that was part of the cultural pattern of the country. There is some justification in Burmese claims that British colonialism, by suppressing initiative, is to blame. Yet this did not alter the need for initiative and for the capacity for decision.

The British had left, too, as a heritage for the Burmese people, the tradition of an opposition without responsibility. The Burmese had been allowed to develop a political opposition to the ruling authority, but not to take action. Naturally, this created an irrational hostility to government and a compromise mentality that encouraged disregard of law and corruption. No overnight grant of democratic privileges from topside down could bring about a democratic behavior pattern.

Insurrection broke out in many parts of the country. U Nu hoped against hope that those who took to the sword were basically patriotic because they were, as he was, of Burmese nationality. He could not bring himself to believe that Burmese would knowingly work in the interests of any foreign power.

The invasion of southern Korea by Communist forces created a new dilemma. That nations calling themselves socialist might actually be impelled by imperialism seemed to turn reason upside-down, and was almost too disillusioning to grasp. He had determined that Burma would steer a middle path, yet as a Burmese patriot he could not ignore unprovoked aggression on another small, Asian country, as had happened in Korea. Burma's turn might come next. So he led Burma bravely into condemnation of the aggres-

sion. With his small land torn by civil strife, this was
as far as he could bring himself to go.

In Parliament, while dogmatic leftists listened
skeptically, he brought home the issue by saying:

> *A small, weak nation like ours, howsoever
> we strengthen our defenses, can never suc-
> cessfully defend ourselves alone . . . as soon
> as aggression started in South Korea, the
> United Nations went to its assistance. This
> has set up a noble precedent. Henceforth, if
> aggression occurs elsewhere, there too the
> United Nations must step in.*

As always, it was the Burmese-minded patriot
speaking. In the same speech, however, he insisted
that Burma would follow a completely non-partisan
policy toward the countries led by Moscow and those
led by Washington. In the past, this effort at eating
one's cake and having it too had proven successful.
Because of world conditions, Burma had achieved the
impossible. U Nu, conditioned by Buddhism, was not
afraid of the impossible; he accepted it casually, as he
did destiny. So far, no matter what the tumble, he had
always landed on his feet, in a firmer stance than before.

He had always had the habit of remaining silent
until he felt that the time had come when an idea boil-
ing up within him required expression, and that the timing was correct, too. This was the practical side to
him. He was not the type to ruin an end by an ill-
chosen word or deed. With a half-dozen small civil
wars raging at once, he had to make haste slowly.

So his speech, on May Day, 1948, boldly entitled

"Warning to Leftists," revealed a confidence that the political maturity of his people — and himself — had advanced sufficiently for him to come out flatly in a manner impossible a short while before:

> *I warn our leftists not to attempt extremes after reading books, but to try and give practical effect to what is possible in the circumstances of our own country.*

That this was an intellectual and a leftist speaking, in the person of the Premier, made this all the more significant. At the same time he quoted Stalin's insistence on building up Russia's own strength first. The inference for Burma could not be missed.

Two years later, his words went farther. He now was being convinced that a doctrinaire Communist owed his allegiance only to Moscow, Burmese by blood or not. At a Resistance Day rally, he talked of wolves in sheep's clothing in Freedom League ranks, declaring:

> *These wolves shout the word "democracy" at the top of their voices when they attack the government. But when they declare their political faith they declare for dictatorship. I will give you a clear picture of the dictatorship they believe in.*
>
> *In a dictatorship country there is only one party ruling, all opposition being ruthlessly suppressed. Criticism of the government is a capital offense. You may not vote freely for the candidates you choose. Information is what the party feeds the masses. Foreign contacts are cut off by the iron curtain.*

> *The task now facing the Anti-Fascist
> People's Freedom League is to combat these
> ogres, new and old, who are about to over-
> whelm the masses with propaganda fumes,
> and then feast on power.*

Burma had been severely wounded by the war.
Rangoon had been smashed by intermittent Axis and
Allied bombing. Cities and towns throughout the country were still a shambles. Everything that was needed
merely for sheer survival was lacking. The officials
charged with rehabilitation programs hardly knew
where to start. Any start could only be so little, compared with the great need.

12

In such a situation, U Nu acted in a very characteristic manner, as probably no other head of state
or government official would have acted, in Burma or
anywhere else. He built a pagoda. In unshakable com-
posure, as placid as the many-armed, eternally merci-
ful Goddess of Mercy, and as unyielding to misfortune
as the immobile Buddha that comforts worshippers in
countless pagodas throughout the country, U Nu built
a vast pagoda, and called it the Peace Pagoda.

He did not do this as a government enterprise,
but as a personal matter, as any Burmese family head
might set up a shrine or temple, small or large. He
could not afford to pay the quarter-million American
dollars that the Rangoon authorities declared it would
cost, so he accepted contributions. This also was in the

Burmese manner. He put the control of the pagoda in the charge of trustees.

Foreign observers were stunned. This money could have built many thousands of homes, and furnished hundreds of thousands of people with clothing. But U Nu realized that even all of this would have been only a drop in the bucket of Burma's great need. For a problem of this vastness, that would take so many years to be successfully tackled, U Nu knew that a nation's morale first had to be fortified. Then nothing was impossible; then anything was possible. So U Nu first built a Peace Pagoda.

He gave the world a startling display of his high motivation in early summer, 1956, after national elections in Burma. He resigned as chief of the government to concentrate all his time to work within his own party, the Freedom League, to rid it of softening and sometimes corrupting influences that had seeped in with prolonged retention of power. He was prompted to take this drastic step when the extreme Leftists won three times as many votes as Burmese observers had anticipated. U Nu knew this was not because of any affection for the Communists; it was disappointment over deflated expectations.

This is the man who, out of Burma's first experiences as a sovereign nation, forged the play, "The People Win Through." U Nu once remarked, in a jocular mood, "If the King of Siam can compose music, why can't I write plays?" Yet this play of his was no mere product of his leisure time, through which he gave vent to his yearning to write. He wrote this play out of a determination to put into words what history was teaching him, so his country could learn the same lessons.

A preface to the published work was contributed by U Thant, a high government official who is a key figure in Burma's Society for the Extension of Democratic Ideals. He wrote:

> The People Win Through *shows what actually happens when Burmese Communists decide to stage an insurrection.*
>
> *On June 18, 1950, a meeting took place at the house of Prime Minister U Nu. U Thein Han, U Nya Na, U Myo Mih, Saya Hein and the writer of this introduction discussed with U Nu the advisability of writing a play depicting the evils of attempting to wrest political power by means of force. After a lengthy discussion covering over three hours, it was decided that U Nya Na should write a play with the following themes:*
>
> *1. How King Narathu, who wrested power by force, fell at the hand of the assassin.*
>
> *2. How Phaung-gar-saw Maung Maung, who wrested power by force, met with the same fate.*
>
> *3. A more up-to-date narrative with similar theme.*
>
> *On August 5, 1950, a second meeting took place at the Prime Minister's house, and U Nya Na's play was examined. It was agreed that the original idea of incorporating three separate incidents in a single play would be unwieldy, and U Nu took over the task of writing a play on one single theme, in his leisure moments. The Prime Minister started writing in August of that year during his tour of the delta regions in his drive, "From Peace to Stability."*

> *On return from the tour, he had finished
> the first two scenes and continued writing
> at odd moments when state duties were less
> pressing. In September the play was com-
> pleted. After the necessary approval had been
> accorded by the Executive Committee of the
> Anti-Fascist People's Freedom League and
> the Council of Ministers to its proposed pub-
> lication, the third meeting of the above gentle-
> men was held on November 4, 1950, and style,
> syntax, etc., were examined. U Nu then kindly
> made over the manuscript, together with its
> copyright, to the Society for the Extension of
> Democratic Ideals.*

Once written, the problem of production remained.
Civil war was raging in the land. If the play had been
performed publicly in Burma, or almost anywhere else
in Asia, there was no doubt that the Communists would
have stopped at no violence to prevent the public from
seeing it. So the play was first distributed in mimeo-
graphed form, and later printed in pamphlet form. The
first performance in Burma was still later over the
radio — an act a week. The reception was gratifying.
The first public showing was in the United States. The
Pasadena Playhouse staged "the People Win Through"
in California early in 1952, in an English version,
which was widely acclaimed. Meanwhile, the Cascade
Pictures Corporation of America filmed the play in
Burma in 1953 with an entirely Burmese cast, giving
it the title, "Rebellion."

The play is now studied in all the Burmese middle
schools. This is the age group to which the Communists make their most calculated appeals. Many a
young student sees himself in the various roles — in
real life. This is as U Nu wanted it.

PROLOGUE

Ladies and gentlemen, I want to say just a few words, but they are very important words.

Our Union of Burma is standing at a cross-roads. One way leads to the seizing of power by force. The other leads to the willing delegation of power by the people to their representatives elected by fair democratic methods.

The first way is not new for Burma. Her kings and usurpers have followed it for two thousand years — parricides, fratricides and others who murder their own kind. So our strength wasted away and at last we found ourselves slaves under a foreign yoke.

Even before this happened our poor common people shrivelled up under the power-lust of those tyrants like lotus flowers in a dried pond. In the struggle for power those who lost had to flee for their lives, or die. Too often innocent people were among the victims.

These tyrants of course cared nothing for the people since they did not depend on them for their power. They thought nothing of cutting a man's head off and confiscating his property. The people lived in fear and trembling.

And what did they do for the people over whom they wielded such absolute power? Nothing; nothing. Generally they were too busy retaining their power. What had been taken by force could only be kept by repression, spying and organized violence.

This evil is now rearing its ugly head in Burma. If this wickedness (may the Lord spare us, friends) — if this wickedness takes hold of our fair country, it will reduce her to a state of abject misery and subjection to tyranny that would beggar description. So we have staged this play, which, I hope, will help you to decide which way to choose.

(Exit)

SCENE I

PLACE: *A house in Rangoon, the home of U Ba Thein, a retired civil servant. He has a son, Aung Win, and a daughter, Ma Hla Myint. Aung Win and his wife, Khin Nwe, have two children, a ten year old boy, Tet Toe, and an eight year old girl, Hla Hla.*

TIME: *An evening in March, 1948, about eight p.m.; U Ba Thein, Ma Hla Myint and Aye Maung are talking in U Ba Thein's living room. Khin Nwe is listening with her little daughter, Hla Hla, asleep on her lap. Tet Toe beside her is also almost asleep with his small chin on the arm of the sofa.*

AYE MAUNG:
Have you any ideas, Sir, about what has come up between Ma Hla Myint and myself?

U BA THEIN:
That's your business. I leave the whole thing to you. Fix it up between yourselves.

AYE MAUNG:
What about as soon as Lent is over?

U BA THEIN:
Just as you like. Talk it over with her.

AYE MAUNG:
The reason I want to set the date early is —

U BA THEIN:
Yes, yes, the sooner the better. I like to get on with
things . . . Besides, I'm getting old, you know. Time to
think of the other world. I've been a bit too easy-going
about that kind of thing. Now that it's getting near
I'm sorry I have been so careless. Live easy, die hard;
live strict, die easy, as the saying goes. I'm thinking
of spending a few months in a retreat, and I'd like
to get your business settled first; so, the sooner, the
better.

AYE MAUNG:
I'd like you to have a word or two with her first.

U BA THEIN:
Why?

AYE MAUNG *(smiling at Ma Hla Myint)*:
After we are married I want Ma Hla Myint to give
up her teaching.

U BA THEIN:
Yes, of course. She ought to realise that housekeeping
is a full-time job.

AYE MAUNG:
There you are, Myint, I told you so.

MA HLA MYINT:
Told me what! You can't put it over on me like that,
Maung. I'm not going to give up my job and live on
other people's earnings. How would you like it if I
insisted that you not practise at the bar?

AYE MAUNG:
Now you're being silly.

U BA THEIN:
Well, you know the pair of them, Aye Maung. It's not
much good talking to them. I suppose it's my fault. I
don't approve of managing children too much. I just tell
them what I think and they can take it or leave it.
No parent can go on looking after his children all
their lives. Start them young to find out for themselves what is right and what is wrong. That way
they'll learn by their mistakes and when they choose
right they'll remember the lesson all their lives.
Look at Aung Win. I wanted him to be a doctor and
he wanted to get into the Civil Service. I didn't interfere. During the Japanese Occupation, too — I
wanted him to sit still and start a little business.
But he wanted to enlist in the Army. I didn't interfere. When he joined the Resistance Movement I
didn't even know about it. And then after the war I
wanted him to settle down in some business, and
what does he do? He becomes a politician, and a Communist at that. I didn't interfere. I never interfere
with my children. It is better for them to paddle
their own canoes and learn from their own experiences.

AYE MAUNG:
So you think Ma Hla Myint shouldn't give up her job.

U BA THEIN:
Let her stick to it so long as she wants to. By the time she's got a few howling brats and a thousand things to worry about around the house, she'll be only too glad to give up teaching. There'll be no need to press her. *(Turning to his wife)* Say, Khin Nwe, what about your children? Isn't it time they went to bed?

KHIN NWE:
They won't go, Father. Their Daddy has promised to take them to the movies, and they're still hoping.

U BA THEIN:
What time is it, Aye Maung?

AYE MAUNG:
Eight-twenty by my watch.

U BA THEIN:
The movies will be over by now. Well, well, children, I'll take you to the movies tomorrow; go to bed now like good children.

(Exit Khin Nwe carrying Hla Hla in her arms with Tet Toe at her elbow.)

U BA THEIN:
Aung Win has been coming home later and later these

nights. You'd better have a word with him, Hla Myint.

AYE MAUNG:

I'm afraid I must let the cat out of the bag. Your son, sir, is going underground. *(U Ba Thein stares uncomprehendingly at him.)* The Communists are planning an insurrection. It's coming off any time now.

U BA THEIN:

But what is this insurrection for? And where did you get the news, Aye Maung? I can't believe it.

AYE MAUNG:

It's true enough.

U BA THEIN:

I don't think it can be and do you know why? About four months ago I said to Aung Win, "Well, son, Burma will soon be independent. What line is your Communist party going to take?" He replied, "Yes, Dad, Independence is coming; but Independence doesn't mean that you have gained all you want. It only means that you are free to work for what you want. Then you still have to work for it. As a matter of fact, Thakin Than Tun and Thakin Nu are putting their heads together to see how they can make this Independence mean something. So they decided to bury the hatchet and so on and just work together for the good of the country." I was so pleased to hear this that I said "Good — good — good." That's why I simply can't understand what you say about an insurrection.

AYE MAUNG:

That *was* the Communist attitude all right four months ago. But do you remember the Communist rally in Calcutta which Thakin Than Tun and his associates went to in the middle of last month?

U BA THEIN:

Yes, I heard something about it.

AYE MAUNG:

At that rally it was resolved that the Communists in all the South East Asian countries start insurrections. This resolution was adopted at the Communist conference in Pyinmana only four or five days ago.

U BA THEIN *(his eyes growing wide with anxiety)*:

No!

AYE MAUNG:

Yes. Since the Pyinmana conference it is quite clear that the Communists have changed their program. At their various gatherings you hear some surprising statements from their leaders. Government seems to have suddenly become anathema to them. It must be brought down by armed insurrection, they say. The masses, they say, must drive Thakin Nu's government out of power just as they would stone a mad dog. They say and write all these things and the Government looks on with folded arms as though it were afraid of them.

U BA THEIN *(staring at Aye Maung for some time)*:

But isn't it just the usual political mud-slinging? I find it hard to believe that these Communists would be so foolish as all that.

AYE MAUNG:
Ah, but Communists are not supposed to form their own judgments. Communist party discipline is such that common sense and judgment go by the board.

U BA THEIN:
I don't follow you. What do you mean exactly?

AYE MAUNG:
Exactly what I said. Communists are not supposed to act on their own judgments. They have to do exactly as they're told. For instance, they know perfectly well that white is white, but their bosses tell them that white is black; and that black is for them. So, white goes over-board.

U BA THEIN:
Look here, Aye Maung. Supposing the instructions issued by their bosses don't fit in with conditions in their own country, must the Communists there still follow them?

AYE MAUNG:
Yes.

U BA THEIN:
Can't they refuse?

AYE MAUNG:
They can't refuse.

U BA THEIN:
Can't they even explain the situation?

AYE MAUNG:
No. Their discipline is as hard as steel and the motto is — "He who is not with us is against us." That makes it very awkward.

U BA THEIN:
Good heavens! This is too much. I just can't believe it.

AYE MAUNG:
It's true all the same. Listen, you were telling me just now, weren't you, how Aung Win mentioned that the Communists meant to work together with the Government to make our Independence good? And two months later Thakin Than Tun and his associates attended the Communist Rally in Calcutta. As soon as they were back they advocated armed insurrection against Thakin Nu's government. Why did they suddenly change? Think it over and decide for yourself.

U BA THEIN:
Wait a minute, Aye Maung. What I want to know is this — is it really true that the Communists in a particular country have to carry out the instructions from the outside, right or wrong, good or bad? If that is so, surely these Communists who don't dare breathe

through their own noses must be the biggest fools in creation.

AYE MAUNG:
They are, they are.

U BA THEIN:
I wonder if it is a coincidence after all, this projected insurrection and the Calcutta rally. Our young politicians are quite hot-headed and thoughtless enough to go off the deep end without instructions from outside.

HLA MYINT:
I find it hard to believe that the Communists have to start a rising under instructions from outside. Surely there are some people with common sense among them.

AYE MAUNG:
I never said there weren't. Didn't you hear what I said?

HLA MYINT:
Well, you say that the Communists have to go into insurrection under instructions from the outside, don't you?

AYE MAUNG:
Yes, well?

HLA MYINT:
Well, then I say, if there are some sensible people

among them, they won't start a rising just because others beat the drum.

AYE MAUNG:
And what then?

HLA MYINT:
What more is there to say?

AYE MAUNG:
Plenty.

HLA MYINT:
Oh, stop it, Ko Aye Maung. Arguing with you is enough to give one a headache.

AYE MAUNG:
You'll make a fine school mistress with such a temper! Why not do all the talking?

HLA MYINT:
I'd never lose my temper if you'd just speak plainly, but I've no patience with a man who twists his words round and round like a lawyer.

AYE MAUNG:
I don't twist my words, Myint, you don't listen to them to the end. All you do is jump to your own conclusions.

HLA MYINT *(stamping her foot)*:
Oh, indeed!

U BA THEIN *(interrupting)*:
Let's hear what Aye Maung has to say, dear. Go on,
Aye Maung.

AYE MAUNG:
All right. I admit there are some sensible people among
the Communists.

HLA MYINT:
There you are. Isn't that enough?

AYE MAUNT and U BA THEIN:
Just a minute, Myint.

AYE MAUNG:
I admit there are sensible people among the Communists but the iron discipline they're under does not
admit independent thought. It only recognizes blind
obedience to instructions from above, so that your
sensible people can't make use of the sense they have.
If their masters say "white," they must say "white,"
or "black," they must say black. If they are told that
black is white, they wouldn't even dare to say it's
rather darkish. If they say it's not quite white they'll
be jumped on and branded as deviationists and traitors
to the world revolution. So there you are, Myint. You
didn't wait for me to explain fully; you just stuck to
your own opinion.

HLA MYINT:
Nonsense! You're making it all up. I don't believe a

word of it. You couldn't get people to behave like that
if you rounded them up and put them in jail. You
might do it with cattle. But you'd need nose rings even
with cows because some of them might kick. So Aye
Maung is just talking nonsense.

AYE MAUNG:
Very well then, that's enough. It's no use saying anything more.

HLA MYINT:
Now who's losing his temper!

AYE MAUNG:
I'm not a bit angry.

HLA MYINT:
Then why did you snap at me?

AYE MAUNG:
It's no use, you won't listen to reason, you just go on
saying the same thing over and over again.

HLA MYINT:
But you yourself said that rebellion is not child's play.
What about that?

AYE MAUNG:
That's just what I said: rebellion is not child's play.
The Communists are quite aware of that. Their text-
books make it very plain, yet in spite of that they're

planning this insurrection. Who is putting them up to it, do you think, if it isn't their foreign bosses?

HLA MYINT:
It might be because of dirty work in the Freedom League.*

AYE MAUNG:
Dirty work in the Freedom League doesn't explain a rebellion. If you'll listen, I'll tell you what a serious business rebellion is.

HLA MYINT:
Don't be too long about it, though, please, teacher.

AYE MAUNG:
Well, in the first place, the Communists themselves know better than anyone how serious rebellion is. It's all explained in their textbooks. For instance, they compare it to a surgical operation. You can't perform it whenever you like. The sore must be ripe; the instruments must be ready and the surgeon must be well-qualified. It isn't like sending for your cook from the kitchen and telling him to have a go at it with a meat chopper. No! It's not likt that. Insurrection has to be properly timed. The Brain Trusts behind the revolution have written it all down in their textbooks. They don't want hot-headed young revolutionaries starting futile

---

* Freedom League is generally referred to by its initials AF-PFL: Anti-Fascist People's Freedom League.

insurrections every now and then. According to them
there are four conditions for a successful revolution —
(telling them off on his fingers one by one)

First — The masses must be seething with discontent under a tyrannical government.

Second — There must remain no other course open
to them except revolution.

Third — There must be able and unimpeachable
leaders.

Fourth — There must be disciplined followers who
are trained in revolution.

So, for a revolution there must be at least these
four conditions. Well, let us see if these conditions exist
here in Burma.

Do the masses hate and abhor the present AFPFL
government? No! *(Looking at U Ba Thein he repeats)*
No! I'm not supporting the AFPFL, mind you. I myself have no high opinion of the AFPFL. They never
had power before and their first taste of it has gone
to their heads and there's no bringing them down to
earth! And, too, there are a good many thieves and
scoundrels among them, who use the AFPFL as a
cover. So long as it harbors such men I can't have
much respect for it. But when it comes to starting a
revolution one must judge by principles and not by
persons. When you think it over you will find the masses
don't hate and abhor the AFPFL government, because
of its principles. Only two months ago, sir, the AFPFL
won Independence for the country. Even if we suppose, for the sake of argument, that the AFPFL government is rotten, how could the masses have discovered its rottenness in two months? They couldn't pos-

sibly. So there isn't mass discontent, and to force a rising when the people are not discontented is like lancing a boil just for the fun of it without waiting until it's ripe.

Next, if this government is rotten, is there no other way to get rid of it but by armed rebellion? Of course there are other ways. Eighteen months from the 4th of January, 1948, the present government must hold a general election. Why not go to the country and put an end to the "rotten" government by constitutional means? I'll bet you, Sir, that if the Communists are so keen on wrecking this government as to start an insurrection they will not wreck the government now but will prolong the process beyond the eighteen months allowed by the Constitution.

Next, look at the leadership of the Communists. It's pretty feeble. Rising against the fascist Japanese is one thing. Rising against one's own national government is quite another. When we rose against the Japanese the whole country was fed up with them, and Japan was demoralized and sick of fighting. Besides, then we had the Allied forces to help us with men and materials, planes, arms, and ammunition. We haven't got all that now and just the little experience we gained in the anti-fascist revolt against the Japanese will not help us much against our own national government.

Then again, there's rivalry and disaffection among the Communist leaders themselves. There are continual recriminations and exposures. We read in the newspapers of Communist leaders who misappropriate funds and rape women. Every one of them stirs up trouble between the men and tries to get more power that way.

You can judge for yourself whether such a dishonest, lustful, jealous gang will make good leaders in a revolution.

Finally, do these Communists have well-trained followers who are ready for revolution? Not yet. Who is it they expect to fight for them? Just dacoits.* Men with barely the pluck to fire a gun are not good revolutionists. Dacoits dare to bully only the weak. Or they fight only to fill their bellies. They are not men to fight and die for an idea.

There you are then. None of the four conditions required to justify a revolution exist in Burma. Even the densest and stupidest Communist leader should realise that Burma is not ripe for revolution. Their leader, Than Tun, knows it, too. The fact that the Communists participated in the last elections and came into the Constituent Assembly; the fact that Communist members of the Assembly supported the Constitution, the fact that they promised (only just before Than Tun went to Calcutta) to work with the government to make our Independence a reality — all these facts prove that they themselves considered that Burma was not yet ripe for revolution. If they had thought it was time for a revolution they would never have accepted these conditions. But their textbooks teach them that if the conditions for a successful revolution are absent they must worm themselves into every possible position within the government itself.

---

* Dacoit: Anyone who goes berserk, particularly referring to members of robber gangs in India and Burma.

You can't come to any other conclusion. It's as clear as daylight that our Communists are not planning an insurrection because they themselves believe that the time has come for a revolution, but because they have had orders from their foreign bosses.

U BA THEIN:
Let me ask you one thing. It's obvious that the time is not ripe for revolution. Then why do the foreign bosses give such foolish orders and why do the men here follow them so blindly?

AYE MAUNG:
As for that, the Big Powers have many ways of exercising pressure on small nations and moving them about like pawns. They play all sorts of tricks to get control over them. When war breaks out between the Big Powers they do all they can to make the small nations their allies or to prevent them from becoming the allies of other nations.

U BA THEIN:
What tremendous power these bosses have! Like heathens who must sacrifice their own children, these Communist "hopefuls" must destroy their own country and make it run with the blood of their own people. What lengths they will go to to please their bosses! Wonderful power!

AYE MAUNG:
Yes, wonderful!

U BA THEIN:

One thing more, Aye Maung. Tell me the truth. Have we signed any treaty with either Soviet Russia or the Anglo-Americans to fight if there is a war? Personally I don't want a war or any kind of fighting for either side. We've suffered enough damage already. Tell me quite plainly if there is any such agreement.

AYE MAUNG:

There can't be, sir.

U BA THEIN:

How can you tell?

AYE MAUNG:

Because, if there were, it would have been laid before Parliament.

U BA THEIN:

Supposing it were a secret treaty and not shown to Parliament?

AYE MAUNG:

Then it would not be a legally binding treaty. The Government can make any treaty with foreign countries but it can do so only on behalf of Parliament. And as it acts on behalf of Parliament it must always table any treaty in Parliament for ratification. If Parliament refuses to ratify a treaty that treaty is void, and the Government falls. Therefore there is no secret treaty. A treaty is legally binding only after ratification. So if war breaks out when there's a secret treaty the

Ministers who made this treaty can get hold of guns and fight, but no one else need join in.

U BA THEIN:
So these insurgents are like two cocks in one coop that start fighting each other just because some one sets them to it. Are the Communists of Burma really so unpatriotic?

AYE MAUNG:
Ah! That's just what riles me. And besides — Oh! Hullo! Here's Aung Win come back *(Aung Win and Boh San Sha, a member of the White Band PVO, or People's Volunteer Organization, enter. Aung Win nods to Aye Maung and goes straight inside followed by Boh San Sha.)*

U BA THEIN:
Hey, Aung Win, come here a minute. *(Aung Win reappears and remains standing.)* Sit down. *(Aung Win sits.)* The children were waiting for you to take them to the movies. I've just sent them to bed with a promise.

AUNG WIN:
Oh, yes, Father, but I had some business to attend to and couldn't make it.

U BA THEIN:
Very well, son. But now that you're back I want to ask you something. Will you give me a straight answer? *(Father and son look at each other.)* Is it true that

you Communists are about to start an insurrection? *(Aung Win remains silent looking at his father blankly.)* I'll speak quite plainly, Aung Win. You are no longer a boy; you have two children and responsibilities. You should think things over carefully before you make decisions. You should do what you feel is right. But as your father it is my duty to warn you when you make mistakes. I am not going to interfere. You must use your own judgment. I'll only say this. If you people go into insurrection you will be making a big mistake, my boy. *(Aung Win gazes into space, saying nothing.)*

AYE MAUNG:
Your father's right, Aung Win. It will be a bad mistake. We've grown up together like brothers, and you know that in the whole course of our friendship I've never once led you astray. So please let me say just this. You'll all be sorry if you start this insurrection.

U BA THEIN *(to Ma Hla Myint)* :
What about getting some dinner for Aung Win, dear. *(Exit Ma Hla Myint.)*

AUNG WIN:
(To Aye Maung) :
But you know those guys in the AFPFL are a bad lot.

AYE MAUNG:
Say they are a bad lot, is that a good enough excuse for a rebellion?

AUNG WIN:

Look what they have done! Haven't they sold the country to the British Imperialists with this "Independence" talk?

AYE MAUNG:

Well, that is a matter for your politicians and the AFPFL to settle between yourselves. I'm not going to interfere. But what I do say is that this insurrection of yours will be a frightful mistake.

AUNG WIN:

We can't let those fellows sell the country like that. We must smash them. Before they declared this so-called Independence our group was quite close to real Independence. Now that the AFPFL and the British Imperialists have pulled this Independence stuff on the masses, real Independence is further off than ever. Would you, Aye Maung, let these enemies of Independence carry on like this without lifting a finger? We can't stand by with folded arms while the AFPFL traitors throw away the Independence which the Resistance fighters bled and died for. Tell me, Aye Maung, do *you* accept this fake independence born out of the Nu-Attlee Agreement drawn up by the British Imperialists and the Quislings? It is all very well for armchair critics to say "It will be a mistake to start a revolution"; "A mistake to do this"; "A mistake to do that"; it's not so easy for a revolutionary to decide what's right and what's wrong. Before you give me your advice answer me one thing. Do you accept this bogus independence?

AYE MAUNG:
Certainly.

AUNG WIN:
You do?

AYE MAUNG:
Yes.

AUNG WIN:
Why?

AYE MAUNG:
Because it is not bogus.

AUNG WIN:
Oh, you idiot! It is so obviously bogus that I am astonished you don't see it. I'm afraid you have been
taken in by AFPFL propaganda.

AYE MAUNG:
There you are! You Communists accuse everybody
who has not fallen for Communist propaganda of having fallen for someone else's propaganda. You label us
all deviationists, traitors and opportunists. That's
why we fight shy of arguing with you.

AUNG WIN:
That's not so. The whole thing is so clear that I
simply don't understand how you can persist in saying
it isn't faked. The facts are staring you in the face.

AYE MAUNG:
What facts?

AUNG WIN:
You know that clause in the Agreement which says that compensation must be paid where British interests are nationalized? How can independence given on that condition be genuine.

AYE MAUNG:
Is that all?

AUNG WIN:
Look at the Defence Agreement, too. It is just like the Anglo-Jordan Agreement which was drawn up to make Jordan a British military base. The Imperialists may shout as loud as they please that they have given Burma independence; these two facts in the Nu-Attlee Agreement prove that what they have given us is a sham. Economically as well as militarily we're bound hand and foot to the Imperialists.

AYE MAUNG:
Is that all?

AUNG WIN:
What do you mean, "is that all?" Isn't that enough?

AYE MAUNG:
To judge from those two facts of yours the independence we've won is certainly genuine. Look at it closely. It speaks for itself.

AUNG WIN:
How do you make that out?

AYE MAUNG:
I've heard all about its being a fake because we've agreed to pay compensation. That's well enough from people who don't know any better, but I can't understand why a man like you with a decent education should think that way.

BOH SAN SHA *(who has joined them)*:
What's all this highbrow talk about a decent education? Why is it so important as all that?

AYE MAUNG *(glancing)*:
Oh, hello, I haven't had the pleasure.

AUNG WIN:
This is PVO Boh San Sha.

AYE MAUNG:
Glad to meet you.

AUNG WIN:
Tell us why you can't understand.

AYE MAUNG:
If compensation detracts from Independence, why did your Soviet Russia pay compensation?

AUNG WIN:
When was that?

AYE MAUNG:
Don't you know? Didn't Soviet Russia annex Petsamo from Finland and then have to pay one hundred and twenty million American dollars to the Canadian Company who owned the nickel mines in Petsamo?

AUNG WIN:
I never heard of Soviet Russia paying any compensation to any one.

AYE MAUNG:
Oh, no! That's the kind of thing you Communists never hear of. You've all got it stuck firmly in your heads that Soviet Russia can never be wrong. You will never hear anything against the Soviets. You couldn't if you tried.

AUNG WIN:
Can you prove to me in print that Soviet Russia did actually pay compensation?

AYE MAUNG:
Don't be so stupid, Aung Win. That sort of transaction is not fixed up between two people privately. A thing like that is known to all the world and his wife. If you want to know how it works I'll explain it to you sometime.

The trouble with you people is your fixed ideas. If you confiscate all foreign property, it's real independence; chuck out all foreign capitalists, it's real independence; sever all connection with the British Imperialists who have exploited the country for the past hundred

years and it's real independence. Fanatics, that's what
you are. And fanaticism always leads to trouble.

Couldn't Soviet Russia have simply confiscated
those nickel mines? She was an independent power and
could confiscate them without consulting any one.
Why didn't she? Because it was in her own interest
to pay compensation. Suppose she confiscated them.
What then? The other powers would retaliate either
by confiscating Soviet property in their own countries or by severing economic relations or by declaring
war. Confiscation wouldn't pay. In this modern world
no country can afford to isolate itself from all economic
and political relations with other countries. All countries are inter-related. Soviet Russia took all that into
account when she decided to pay compensation and
that is why Burma agreed to pay compensation. Don't
run away with the idea that just because you are independent you can start defying other countries.
America, Britain and even Russia cannot afford to
ride rough-shod over international relations, let alone
a tiny land like ours. There is such a thing as common
interest. Modern countries have to follow the policy of
give-and-take with an eye on the common interest.
Fanaticism won't do. Even you people will learn these
things when you actually have to run a country.

U BA THEIN:
Aye Maung, you haven't answered Aung Win's charge
that our Defence Agreement is the same as the Anglo-
Jordan Agreement which was drawn up to make Jordan
a British military base.

AYE MAUNG:
Ah, yes. Aung Win is not quite up to date. His own leaders, Thakin Than Tun and Goshal, have dropped this accusation since Thakin Nu's recent public explanation.

U BA THEIN:
How did Thakin Nu explain it?

AYE MAUNG:
You must have missed the news in the papers.

U BA THEIN:
I must have.

AYE MAUNG:
It happened like this. Than Tun and Goshal were declaiming against this Anglo-Jordan Agreement of Aung Win's so persistently that Thakin Nu invited Thakin Than Tun and Goshal to come and have it out with him. When they came Thakin Nu said to them, "I have here a copy of the Anglo-Jordan Agreement. You have been shouting from the house-tops that our Defence Agreement and the Anglo-Jordan Agreement are the same. Have you read the Anglo-Jordan Agreement?" Than Tun and Goshal admitted that they hadn't. They had only read a review of it. Then Thakin Nu handed over his copy of the Anglo-Jordan Agreement to them. Since then no more was heard about this alleged similarity from Than Tun and Goshal.

U BA THEIN:

My dear Aung Win, what kind of leaders are they?
Funny their saying that without even having read
the Trans-Jordan treaty. It just made them look foolish. If leaders go off the path their followers will lose
it altogether. Eh, Aye Maung?

AYE MAUNG:

Quite. As a matter of fact the defence clause in the
Nu-Attlee Agreement about which they are making
such a hullabaloo is this: The Government of the
Union of Burma invites a British Military Mission to
Burma. This Mission will be in Burma in order to give
military training to our Army. But after three years
we can send it back by giving twelve months' notice.
That's one point.

The second point is that the Union Government
agrees to give appropriate assistance to the British Mission which comes to help us. Of course, if we agree to accept British Military assistance, we must assist the
British forces which come to our assistance. That's all
there was to it. And with these two minor points the
Communists started to shout that our defence agreement was just like the Anglo-Jordan Agreement, that
our Defence has been handed over completely to the
British and so on and so on. I just can't figure out how
they could twist these two minor points into such an
accusation.

Please let me tell you a funny story. These Communists remind me of an old lady, Daw Khin, who lived in
our street. She had a son, who was always fighting with
the son of her neighbor, Daw Mya, so that Daw Khin
and Daw Mya also were always at dagger points. One

day Daw Khin's husband came home and told her that the two lads were at it again, that this time it was more serious and that one of them had got his head broken in. Immediately Daw Khin was up in arms and hurled streams of abuse at Daw Mya. She wanted to know what right this good-for-nothing son of good-for-nothing parents had to do that kind of thing. There was no stopping her until her husband whispered to her, "It's *her* son whose head was broken," whereupon she complained it was all his fault for not telling her sooner. Communists are like that. They never study anything carefully. All they think of is to strike out at the other party; they never wait to learn the facts.

Aung Win, as your best friend I tell you that you Communists act first and think later. You know that this insurrection business is no joke. So I do hope that in such a grave matter as this it will not be a case of acting first and thinking afterwards. (*They are silent for about half a minute. Aung Win seems thoughtful and the other two look at him anxiously.*)

BOH SAN SHA (*to Aye Maung*):
If your independence is genuine can your AFPFL Government declare war on the Anglo-Americans?

AYE MAUNG:
You can answer that question yourself. You don't need an answer from me.

BOH SAN SHA:
How can I answer it myself?

AYE MAUNG:

Is there a clause in the Nu-Attlee Agreement stating that Burma must not declare war on the Anglo-Americans? If so, where is it? That you can answer for yourself. *(Boh San Sha is silent.)*

AYE MAUNG:

But look here, Boh, — what's your name?

AUNG WIN:

Boh San Sha.

AYE MAUNG:

Oh, yes; look, Boh San Sha, what on earth do you want to declare war on the Anglo-Americans for? We'd only get smashed up.

BOH SAN SHA:

Why should we get smashed up?

AYE MAUNG:

Well! Look at the strength of the Anglo-Americans and look at what we've got — one obsolete frigate, the *Mayu*, half a dozen MLs fit only to fight in canals and creeks, and half a dozen fighter planes. To declare war with no more than that is *asking* to be smashed up.

BOH SAN SHA:

I don't mean declaring war like that.

AYE MAUNG:
What do you mean then by declaring war?

BOH SAN SHA:
Just a token declaration.

AYE MAUNG:
What on earth do you mean by a "token" declaration?

BOH SAN SHA:
Just declare war but don't actually fight.

AYE MAUNG:
Oh, I see! ! !

BOH SAN SHA:
I want the world to know that we are declaring war on the capitalists. That's why I want a token declaration of war. I shall be quite satisfied with the declaration. No need to go and fight them.

AYE MAUNG:
Dear, dear! That's a bit too deep for me. I've never heard of two ways of declaring war. I've only heard of declaring war to fight. I've never read or heard of a token declaration.

BOH SAN SHA:
If your independence is real, you can do what you like, can't you? You can declare real war or you can make a token declaration of war, whichever you like. You are

free to do what you like. As for these AFPFL fellows, they wouldn't even dare to declare a token war, or even think of it.

AYE MAUNG *(bored with San Sha, turning to Aung Win)*:
Well, Aung Win, think over carefully what I've been saying.

U BA THEIN *(walking up to Aung Win and putting his hand on his shoulder)*:
My boy, you must not join in the rising. In all your life I've never tried to prevent you from doing anything. I must this time. You realize by now how my heart is set against this insurrection business. Will you give me a promise? . . . You know so well how I have always let both of you have your own way. This time do, please, dear lad, let me have mine. Don't turn this great sorrow on me in my old age. Do, please, let me die with an easy mind. *(Aung Win remains silent.)*

AYE MAUNG:
As for me, I don't say that people never ought to rebel. If there's no other way to help the people, then rebel. But there is to be a general election in sixteen months. Then you'll have a chance to smash them. If you think these AFPFL people are such rotters and that your program is better for the people than theirs, you can fight them in the election. Call on the people to decide. Then you'll get honest men instead of rotters and your good program instead of their bad program. If you really believe in your honest leaders

and sound principles you needn't be afraid to fight.
If you start an insurrection when the elections are so
near, then whatever you may say, people will think
that it is because you dare not contest in the election
because you know you will lose.

U BA THEIN:
That is exactly it, my boy. Tell me, Aye Maung, however
strong the AFPFL may be now they must hand over
their power to the party with the most votes, mustn't
they? If the Communists get a majority the AFPFL
must hand over to them?

AYE MAUNG:
Of course!

U BA THEIN:
Suppose they lose the election and then don't resign?

AYE MAUNG:
Ah, that is impossible. In the third section of the Constitution it is definitely stated, "The Sovereignty of the
Union resides in the people." They can't go against
that.

U BA THEIN:
Supposing they won't resign whatever the Constitution says. If you once have power it's not so easy to
give it up.

AYE MAUNG:
No, that's quite impossible. Do you think it is because

of the handful of ministers in this Government that
the people obey its laws, accept its decisions and sub-
mit to its authority? Not at all, sir. It is because the
people themselves have entrusted these ministers with
power. So long as the people support it, so long will
this Government stand; the day they withdraw, then
it falls. The handful of ministers becomes just a handful of ordinary citizens. Who will recognize them as
the Government? If they clung to power without the
mandate of the people I myself would be the first to
join in smashing them. There would be nothing else
to do but to rebel. If they flout the Constitution and
democratic principles, not only the Communists but
the whole nation would rise up against them.

U BA THEIN:

There you are, my boy. Rebellion isn't the only way
by which your party can come into power. If it should
become impossible to gain power by democratic means,
then rebel if you please. But now, my dear son, you
must listen to what I say, you must not join the rebels
before the elections.

AYE MAUNG:

I'll venture, Sir, to make a prediction. If the Communists make proper arrangements during the next
eighteen months they may win the election. But as for
starting a rebellion the conditions are unripe, the Communist leaders are unfit, and the Communist forces
are unready. They won't gain power but they'll gain
the hatred of the whole country. So far from driving
the AFPFL that they call so rotten out of power, they

are more likely to help them into power beyond the eighteen months allowed by the Constitution. You just wait and see.

U BA THEIN:
Dear lad, do promise me you won't take part in the insurrection. I've always let you have your own way; you know that, don't you, son? I can't let you have your way in this. Please don't make me miserable at my age. I want to die in peace, my son.

SERVANT *(enters with a letter for Aung Win)*:
A man just came and asked me to deliver this to you at once, sir. He says it's very urgent.
(Aung Win opens it and reads.)

HLA MYINT *(entering)*:
Dinner is ready, Ko Aung Win.

U BA THEIN:
Is it as late as all that! Go and have your dinner, son. You really mustn't join the rebels. I simply can't allow it. Run along now and have your food. Dinner's ready and it's getting very late.

AUNG WIN *(still reading the letter)*:
All, right, father.

KHIN NWE *(enters in a hurry)*:
Darling, I don't know what has come over little Hla Hla. She is quite feverish.

AUNG WIN *(looking up from his letter)* :
Yes, yes, darling, I'll look at her as soon as I come back. I must be off now and see about something. *(Making to go out.)*

U BA THEIN :
Come, lad! What about your dinner? It's so late already.

AUNG WIN *(going out)* :
Yes, yes, Father, I'll be right back. *(Exit Aung Win and Boh San Sha. U Ba Thein is left gazing after them. He sits motionless with tears running down his cheeks. While everybody in the room watches him in pity, the curtain slowly descends.)*

SCENE II

PLACE: *The reading room of a village in Pegu District, converted into Communist Headquarters after the Communist occupation of the village.*

TIME: *The beginning of April, 1948. In the room are Aung Win, Chit Tun, Boh Tauk Tun and two Red soldiers sitting down to a meeting with four or five villagers who are seated opposite them.*

AUNG WIN:
Have all the village representatives arrived?

HEADMAN:
Only one more, our school teacher, Mg Po Seik. He ought to be here now. *(Getting up and looking out of the door.)*

AUNG WIN:
Will you speak first, Boh Tauk Tun?

BOH TAUK TUN:
I'm a soldier not a speech-maker. No speaking for me.

HEADMAN *(returning to his seat)* :
Mg Po Seik is here. *(Mg Po Seik enters.)*

AUNG WIN :
Well, headman, are you all here now?

HEADMAN :
Yes, all of us.

AUNG WIN :
We have invited you as representatives of the village,
just to straighten things out. Under the leadership of
the Communist party we have now started an armed
revolution. Our one object is to destroy the present
AFPFL Government and set up a People's Government.

Perhaps you have been deceived by the AFPFL's
claims of gaining independence and doing this and
doing that. The fact is that the AFPFL is a wolf in
sheep's clothing. Today I shall show you what this
terrible wolf really is.

Freedom is never won without fighting. Imperialists are all money-grabbers. Remember that. Don't
think they would give back a country as rich as Burma
for nothing. Why, you couldn't even get a bone for a dog
out of them. Well, then, why do they go around shouting that they have put power in the hands of the
AFPFL Government? I'll tell you.

The revolution began in the days of U Ottama and
had been gathering force step by step — Saya San's Rebellion, the Students' Movement, the Workers' Movement, the Anti-British Movement, the Anti-Fascist

Movement. By the end of the Second World War our great revolution had never been so prosperous and never been so powerful. The British Imperialists began to shiver in their boots. They saw that at the rate things were going they would soon be turned out, lock, stock and barrel. So they tried to get stooges to help them by sprinkling around their "independence" eye-wash. It was nothing but a conjuring trick. You know what a conjurer can do. He makes you think he is putting coins or something into your pocket. Then he says that he has given you a present. You believe him. But when you feel in your pocket you find nothing there.

The British Imperialists wanted to play a trick like that on us. To help them they needed people who would be willing to be their stooges. Looking around they found the AFPFL. Have any of you ever read the Nu-Attlee treaty that gave us this so-called Independence? It's just a blind to deceive us Burmans. You may think it gives us independence, because you only look at the outside without troubling to study what's inside. It hands over all our army, lock, stock and barrel, and all our wealth to the British Imperialists and leaves us merely the husk without the grain. Just as our glorious revolution was on the very point of getting real, hundred-per-cent Independence, the AFPFL sold it for the husks and now, taking the husks for the real thing, the people have lost their keenness that inspired our insurrection. It is very nearly dead. With the help of the AFPFL stooges the British Imperialists have played this conjuring trick on us and now real Independence that we so nearly won is farther away than ever. If we don't want to lose it altogether we must first fight the AFPFL who sold out, who are the chief obstacles to Independence, the AFPFL who are the spies and stooges of the British Imperialists. If we don't fight for Independence we shall never win it. That's why the Burma Communist Party is leading this armed insurrection.

No one now has a word to say in favour of the AFPFL. Not the workers, not the peasants. Not the people, not the students, not the clerks, not the officials. They have no one behind them. The AFPFL is crumbling. There won't be any need for fighting; everything will be quite simple. Every one who wants real independence is flocking to our flag and our insurrection is sure of victory. Now those of you who have any questions to ask may do so.

PO SEIK *(standing up in spite of headman's efforts to prevent him from doing so)* :
But if this mighty AFPFL is breaking down by itself why should we want to raise guns to shoot it down? According to the Constitution there must be a general election within fifteen months from today. If there is no one to back it, it will just topple over.

AUNG WIN :
That's AFPFL talk.

BOH TAUK TUN *(pulling out his revolver and pointing it at Po Seik)* :
Are you a member of the AFPFL? *(Aung Win tries to*

grab the revolver but Boh Tauk Tun shoves him aside and keeps it pointed at Po Seik) Tell the truth, you! Are you a member of the AFPFL or not? We've a short way with traitors. We wipe them out.

AUNG WIN:
Steady, Boh Tauk Tun.

BOH TAUK TUN:
Shut up, you. I know my job. *(Turning again on Po Seik.)* Did you hear me? Are you a member of the AFPFL?

PO SEIK *(much surprised)*:
No, I'm not.

BOH TAUK TUN:
Then why did you ask that question?

PO SEIK:
But, Captain, that speaker there *(pointing at Aung Win)* said if we had any questions, to ask them.

BOH TAUK TUN:
Why did you say the kind of thing the AFPFL say?

PO SEIK:
I don't know and I don't care what the AFPFL say. All I know is that it will cause a lot of unnecessary suffering if you fight to crush the AFPFL when it could so easily be done by an election.

BOH TAUK TUN *(stamping his foot)* :
There you go again! Shut up, or I'll shoot you on the
spot. *(The headman pulls Mg Po Seik down to his
seat.)*

AUNG WIN *(leaving his chair and approaching Boh
Tauk Tun with an unhappy air)* :
Come now, Bo Tauk Tun, the whole idea of a revolution is that what it must chiefly aim at is the good
opinion and approval of the people. Don't start off by
turning them against us. That would be a bad job.

BOH TAUK TUN *(to his Red soldiers)* :
Comrades, search this village for the Pro-AFPFL
traitors. Give me a list of them as soon as possible . . .
(Noise of machine-gun fire off-stage) Ha! What's that?
(Chit Tun picks up a gun and goes out.) Comrades,
get out and see. *(He himself goes to the door. The sound
of firing gets louder and nearer. The villagers rush out
by a side door. Boh Tauk Tun runs back into the
room.)* The Government forces are closing in on the
village. *(The sound of firing is now very close).*

CHIT TUN *(off stage)* :
Oh, I'm hit! *(He re-enters limping.)*

AUNG WIN *(running to his help)* :
Where are you hit, Chit Tun?

CHIT TUN :
My leg.

AUNG WIN *(to Boh Tauk Tun who has picked up a*

carbine and is standing in one place, terror-stricken) :
Please take Chit Tun's other arm and we'll carry him
out. *(Heavier rifle fire nearby.)*

BOH TAUK TUN:
The bastards are upon us. No time for this nonsense.
Run for it. *(He runs out, carbine in hand. Aung Win
looks at his receding back, grinds his teeth and clenches
his fist. He carries Chit Tun out with difficulty. The
rifle-fire continues. After the room has been empty a
while, Boh Aye, a platoon commander, and four soldiers
of the Union Forces, the regular army, enter.)*

BOH AYE *(to the soldiers)* :
Search the room, see what you can find. *(He sits down
at the table and examines the files on it.)*

A SOLDIER *(searching in one corner)* :
Look what I've found!

OTHER SOLDIERS *(in unison)* :
What?

1ST SOLDIER:
Cigarettes and whisky. *(Holding them up.)*

2ND SOLIDER *(joining him and rummaging in the box)* :
Well, I'll be . . . Biscuits! Butter! Condensed milk!

3RD SOLDIER *(who has joined them)* :
These Communists set up a Welfare State even before
they've finished their insurrection.

1ST SOLDIER *(to the Platoon Commander)* :
Am I to confiscate these things, sir?

BOH AYE:
These Communists must have been preying on this
village for quite a while. The people are likely to be in
a pretty bad way. Hla Thoung, go and fetch a couple
of villagers to take these things along to the headman's
house. Maung Lin, make a list of them. Pe Mya, take
down that portrait of Stalin and the flag from the wall.
Sein Maung, tie up these files carefully and bring them
along. *(They all comply.)*

SEIN MAUNG *(who is tying up the files)* :
Among these Communist insurgents there is one Ba
Ni, a friend of mine, who often used to drop in for a
chat with me before this trouble started. He used to
say, "This Nga Nu's Government is responsible for
keeping British Imperialism in Burma. To drive it
out we must first drive out the Nga Nu Government."
He said the same thing over and over. He was always
trying to persuade me to join the Communists.

BOH AYE:
Were you ever tempted?

SEIN MAUNG:
Oh, no! I know nothing about politics. I believe only
in one thing. Governments should be made by elections,
and unmade by elections. There's nothing to be gained
by an insurrection; it's looking for lice on a bald
man's head. Am I right, Boh Aye?

BOH AYE:
You say you know nothing about politics, but you seem to have a pretty good grasp of it.

SEIN MAUNG:
No, thanks! No politics for me. Some of these politicians have already got into the army! First it's "Rebel"; then it's "Don't rebel." If I listened to all they say I'd find myself a deserter instead of a soldier.

BOH AYE:
Umm . . . *(Hla Thoung and two villagers enter).*

HLA THOUNG:
Here are the men you wanted, sir.

BOH AYE:
Read me your list, Po Lin.

PO LIN *(reading)*:
Whisky, four bottles; Goldflake cigarettes, nine packets; biscuits, three tins; butter, two tins; condensed milk, twelve tins; cocoa, three tins; coffee, four tins; gramophone records, twenty-two discs; needles, three packets; powder, three tins. That's the lot, sir.

BOH AYE *(to the villagers)*:
Will you take these along to the headman's house with this list? We'll be along in a minute. *(Exit villagers carrying the boxes.)*

HLA THOUNG *(looking enviously after the departing villagers)*:

And we poor bastards in the army are always left to
starve! What's the price of a glass of that whisky and
a Goldflake to smoke with it!

BOH AYE *(affectionately)* :
Don't worry, I'll buy some for you, my lad. Well now,
boys, fall in. I've a few words to say. *(They fall in.)*

BOH AYE *(facing them)* :
I know well enough that you're always short of
these things. It isn't because I don't know ways we
men with guns could live like lords. That would be very
easy. It's much too easy for soldiers to get things since
almost everyone is too frightened of a man with a gun
to refuse him. We soldiers know how to get what we
want and that's why we should watch ourselves when
there's a chance of looting. It's only half true to say that
anyone who can fight will make a soldier. A soldier
must be full of pluck and courage in the face of the
enemy and willing to fight hard, but he must also be
full of sympathy and compassion when he is dealing
with people weaker than himself. The soldier who
fights hard against the enemy should be equally gentle
with the feeble, not ranting and bullying because he
knows no one will stand up to him. The soldier who
stands firm against the enemy's shot and shell should
be equally firm against the temptations of loot and lust.
That's what a soldier is. If a soldier is only good for
fighting and hasn't got these other qualities then there's
no difference between him and so much ammunition.
He's sound without substance, a nut without a kernel,
an ox that can draw a cart, but can't get a calf. Well,

Hla Thoung, for the sake of a few drinks and smokes
do you want to be just so much ammunition, a nut
without a kernel, a bullock that can't breed . . . or do
you want to be a loyal soldier with all the people for
your friends? It's up to you to choose. *(Boh Aye dis-
misses them and moves towards the door. From there
he looks back at Hla Thoung with a smile and asks)*
Have you chosen?

HLA THOUNG *(smiling sheepishly)* :
Yes, sir.

BOH AYE :
Which?

HLA THOUNG :
Well, sir, I'm a man. I would never consent to become
a gelded bullock. I choose to remain a soldier of the
Union.

BOH AYE :
That's right.

(Curtain)

SCENE III

A week later. Four or five village elders and the head-man are talking in the headman's house.

HEADMAN:
That was a pleasant young officer in command of the Government forces.

1ST VILLAGER:
You can always tell a gentleman.

HEADMAN:
If it hadn't been for him there would be nothing left of our village by this time.

1ST VILLAGER:
How do you mean?

HEADMAN:
Why, even without his asking, weren't there four or five dirty sneaks giving tips about who collected food-packets for the Communists, who waited hand-

and-foot on the Communist leader, who went around
with the Communists confiscating arms, and so on?

1ST VILLAGER:
And he didn't take any action on it?

HEADMAN:
None. He took no notice of them and said it was only
natural for people to be frightened with the enemy so
close.

1ST VILLAGER:
But he did arrest Aye Hla's son, Mya Than.

HEADMAN:
Don't you know about Mya Than? It was he who gave
information to the Red leader, Boh Tauk Tun, about
the gold belonging to Miganpa Chettya and U Tha
Maung's. And he stole the lot — even a tiny ring from
U Tha Maung's little son. The schoolmaster, Po Seik,
reported it to the young officer and when he arrested
and questioned Mya Than it all came out.

1ST VILLAGER:
God help Po Seik if the Communists come back.

HEADMAN:
There's no one like Po Seik. He would stand up for
what he thinks is right, even if it cost him his life.

HEADMAN:
I wonder if the Communists know already that the
Union forces have left?

1ST VILLAGER:
Why, they left only last evening. The Communists
couldn't possibly know yet.

2ND VILLAGER:
Don't you believe it! The Communists have spies all
over. If you ask me, they had news of it yesterday as
soon as the soldiers left.

1ST VILLAGER:
If they had they would have been here long ago.

2ND VILLAGER:
That's all right! The Communists are brave enough
to bully unarmed villagers but dare not come anywhere near Government troops. They won't be in a
hurry to come back. They will wait until the Government Forces are well away.

3RD VILLAGER:
What I'm worrying about is that our village might
catch it both ways. Between two fires, you know.

1ST VILLAGER:
How do you mean?

3RD VILLAGER:
The Communists take the village, the troops attack,
the Communists run away. Then the troops leave, the
Communists return, the troops attack again. So it goes
on until nothing is left of the village.

1ST VILLAGER:
That's very likely.

3RD VILLAGER:
What I want to ask is this: if they don't like this Government they can change it by the election, and the election must be held within eighteen months from Independence Day. Why then do they want an insurrection?

1ST VILLAGER:
Just ask them yourself when they're back.

3RD VILLAGER:
Oh, no, no, no! Tell me to catch a tiger by the tail and I won't mind tackling it. But for God's sake don't make me ask the Communists any questions.

1ST VILLAGER:
Are you as frightened of them as all that?

3RD VILLAGER:
Why, yes! Since I heard what happened to Po Seik the other day my knees have been wobbly and a cold shiver runs down my back.

1ST VILLAGER:
The leaflets they distribute say it's because the AFPFL Government interferes with the freedom of speech, the freedom of the press, the freedom of meeting.

3RD VILLAGER:

It's not what they say that frightens me, but what they do. When they called for questions the other day, as soon as Po Seik asked a question, they had their guns up and threatened to shoot him.

4TH VILLAGER:

The way I see it is this: The Communists tell us that they will distribute land freely to us peasants. Very well; if we can put up with small annoyances we shall get free land. "No pain, no gain" as the saying goes. After all, the Communists didn't really do any harm. They merely pointed a gun and did not actually shoot. Don't make a mountain out of a mole-hill. It's a small matter compared with the promise to distribute land.

3RD VILLAGER:

It's not only the Communists who will give out land. Why, our own Government has already passed a Land Nationalization Act.

1ST VILLAGER:

By the time the Communists give out the land there'll be nothing left of the villages but ashes and nothing left of us but bones.

4TH VILLAGER:

Distribution of land by our Government will only happen after compensation and if the Government gives it out, what with compensation to the landlords and so on, there'll be no end to it. Sharp work, soon over — that's what I like.

1ST VILLAGER:
We're not there yet; carry on.

4TH VILLAGER:
Eh?

1ST VILLAGER:
Presto! Confiscated.
   Presto! Give it out.
   Presto! Soldiers come.
   Presto! Communists run and there we are with the
village a heap of ashes.

4TH VILLAGER:
But they only run now because they haven't won yet.

HEADMAN:
It's just because they haven't won that they can bag
the land and dole it out.

4TH VILLAGER:
What do you mean?

HEADMAN:
All politicians are just like that. *Before* they get into
the Government they've got no responsibility for what
they say and what they do. The moment they get into
office they quiet down. If they go on playing the fool
the people will not stand it. Nor will foreign governments. At present these Communists are rebels, if foreign governments suffer any damage the most they

do is complain to the Union Government. That's why the Communists look so brave.

1ST VILLAGER:
As a Buddhist I believe in paying a fair price for what you take.

2ND VILLAGER:
I don't mind waiting if I get what I want, but I want to get it peaceably. I would like to buy a diamond ring, but snatch it from the jaws of a tiger — no, thank you! *(Rifle fire offstage.)*

1ST VILLAGER:
Hah! The Communists!

3RD VILLAGER:
Sssh! Mum, all of you. Don't talk!

2ND VILLAGER *(in a hushed voice)*:
Headman, you've still got the whisky and cigarettes and stuff the young officer handed over?

HEADMAN:
Yes. He meant for me to distribute them among the villagers, but I haven't so much as touched them. I thought I might as well keep them a while just in case the Communists come back.

2ND VILLAGER:
Very wise. Just as well you can look ahead or you'll be in hot water. *(Enter Boh Tauk Tun followed by*

Aung Win and half a dozen Red troopers bearing arms.)

BOH TAUK TUN:
Is the headman here?

HEADMAN:
Yes, Captain.

BOH TAUK TUN:
Any of those Government bastards left in your village?

HEADMAN:
None, Captain. They've all gone.

BOH TAUK TUN:
Did they bully you people?

HEADMAN:
No.

BOH TAUK TUN:
Nonsense! Of course they did.

HEADMAN:
Oh well, perhaps just a little.

BOH TAUK TUN:
Then tell me what they did.

HEADMAN:
Can't say, Captain. I was minding my own business.

BOH TAUK TUN:
You old fool! You've got no bloody guts. How long
do you mean to go on licking the shoes of the Government?

(The Headman looks down in silence.)

BOH TAUK TUN:
Why did the soldiers nab Mya Than?

HEADMAN:
I don't know the whole story, Captain; they said they
were going to investigate some case or other against
him.

BOH TAUK TUN:
Were you among those who reported Mya Than?

HEADMAN:
I swear I had nothing to do with it. May the earth
open up and swallow me if I'm not speaking the truth!

BOH TAUK TUN:
Is it true that Po Seik reported him?

HEADMAN:
I really don't know anything about it.

BOH TAUK TUN:
Speak the truth, old man. *(Drawing his revolver)* I'm
not going to be fooled. Do you want to die on the spot?

Wasn't it Po Seik who went and reported to the soldiers?

HEADMAN:
Captain, if I must die I must die. But you can't make me tell you what I know nothing about.

BOH TAUK TUN:
Call yourself a headman and you know nothing about this! Do you expect me to believe that?

HEADMAN:
I am a very timid man, Captain. Whoever orders me to do anything I do it as best I can. I try to live quietly at home. I really don't know much about what's going on. If you don't believe me, ask anyone. We are only dust beneath your feet. We put up with anything we've got to.

BOH TAUK TUN *(turning to the other village elders)*
What about you people? Can any of you tell me about Po Seik making a report?

(No one replies. They all look down.)

BOH TAUK TUN:
You're a fine lot. Hear nothing — see nothing — say nothing — hah, hah, hah! *(Enter a Red soldier leading Po Seik whose wrists are tied together with ropes. Boh Tauk Tun glares at Po Seik.)*

BOH TAUK TUN:
Hey! You! Did you report Mya Than to the soldiers?

PO SEIK *(facing him firmly)*:
Yes!

BOH TAUK TUN:
Yes, it is! Comrades, take him out and shoot him.

AUNG WIN:
Wait a minute, Boh Tauk Tun —

BOH TAUK TUN:
Don't interfere with me, Aung Win.

AUNG WIN:
What do you think you're doing, Boh Tauk Tun? You can't go shooting people at random for nothing.

BOH TAUK TUN:
Why not?

AUNG WIN:
But you can't go around shooting people!

BOH TAUK TUN:
Mind your own business. I'd have you shot if necessary. You fellows, take him out. Didn't you hear what I said?

AUNG WIN:
Wait! Wait a minute!

BOH TAUK TUN *(pointing his revolver at Aung Win)*:
Be careful, you! Hurry up, you men. *(Getting angrier and angrier.)*

AUNG WIN:
Shoot me if you like but let me ask one thing. *(Turning to Po Seik)* What did Mya Than do which made you report him?

PO SEIK:
Mya Than did Boh Tauk Tun's dirty work for him.

BOH TAUK TUN *(throwing Po Seik out)*:
That's enough of your damn lip.

PO SEIK *(offstage)*:
You gangsters! You dacoits! Take your chance then while you can.

(Noises of Po Seik being hustled away.)

AUNG WIN *(staring at Boh Tauk Tin in amazement)*:
So you've been at it again! Robbing and stealing.

BOH TAUK TUN:
It's none of your business.

AUNG WIN:
It is my business to prevent this kind of business.

BOH TAUK TUN:
Oh, go to hell! How else do you think I'm to feed my

men? You don't do it. It's we who risk our lives and do the fighting. You don't. It's all very well for you to put on a dog's collar and come strutting around here with your "When did you go looting?" and "This is my business." Don't come swanking around here. You're not my boss and I'm not going to stand for it.

AUNG WIN:
I can't agree to all this rough and ready shooting.

BOH TAUK TUN:
Well, if you don't agree, die if you dare. *(Aung Win is speechless for a minute. He heaves a big sigh and gazes into space. Then turning to Bo Tauk Tun again.)*

AUNG WIN:
Think, Boh Tauk Tun. If you go on shooting people you will be making a big mistake.

BOH TAUK TUN:
What do you know about it? Why did the Paris Commune fail? Because they did not kill enough people. It's not I who's making a big mistake. You remember what Lenin said: "Kill, if there's anyone to kill off; don't be soft. Kill him ruthlessly."

(A shot rings out off-stage.)

BOH TAUK TUN *(looking around at all those present in the headman's house)*:
Did you hear that? Let this be a lesson to you. Everyone who tries to curry favour with the Government

will go just the same way. Keep that in your minds. *(He strides out of the house. Aung Win is staring blankly at nothing. The others remain cowed and heavy-hearted, their sighs can be heard from a long distance.)*

Curtain

SCENE IV

PLACE: *The outskirts of a village.*

TIME: *April, 1949. Behind a defensive bunker two men, Aye Nyein and Tha San, are lying prone on the ground. They belong to the White Band PVO which is against both Communists and government. Their rifles are on the parapet, their eyes are scanning the middle distance.*

AYE NYEIN:
I say, Tha San, would you like to read that leaflet I picked up yesterday?

THA SAN:
What leaflet?

AYE NYEIN:
You know those leaflets dropped outside the village.

THA SAN:
Oh, yes, I was told that a man dropped them and disappeared. I haven't seen one.

AYE NYEIN:
I read it yesterday and it almost made me laugh hard enough to split my sides. Listen, I'll read it to you.

THA SAN:
Better wait until we're back in the village. It'll be a bit awkward if those fellows take this chance to surprise us.

AYE NYEIN:
But those territorials* aren't so damn sharp. Listen— *(reads)* "Communism in China and Communism in Burma are not the same thing. Chinese Marxism is a natural growth. The kind of thing that Thakin Than Tun and Thakin Soe call Communism is out of place in Burma. It's all cut and dried dogma imported from abroad and they try to cram it down our throats by force. It is not Marxism. It is murder-ism." *(Sporadic rifle fire in the distance. Occasionally a hand grenade explodes followed by a volley. Tha San grips his rifle and takes cover.)*

AYE NYEIN:
They're miles away. They can't touch us. I'll go on reading.

THA SAN *(peering in the direction of the rifle fire)*:
Wait until we are back at the village, Aye Nyein. If they surprise us we'll lose our lives for nothing.

AYE NYEIN:
That's all right. You keep your eyes on those blighters.

---

* Refers to Burma Territorial Force (BTF), emergency troops raised by the new nation after attaining independence.

I'll just read the extracts about Thakin Soe and Thakin Than Tun. It's wonderful stuff. I was tickled to death reading it last night. *(Reading)*:

THAKIN SOE

1. Thakin Soe is a dying taper which flares up just before going out.

2. He is a second Nga Saung.

3. From boyhood he has been wanted for murder and banditry.

4. His hobbies are fiddling and womanizing. He spends his time lechering and lecturing.

5. He doesn't care how many of his men get killed in his misbegotten revolution while all the time he himself hops into bed with his women, and even with other men's wives. Take what did during the Anti-Japanese Resistance movement. He got a wireless set out of the allies and then used it to send signals for supplies of lipstick, blouses, wrist-watches and other delights for the girls he was busy seducing when he should have been fighting the Japanese. He dawdled away his time with four pet bitches.

THA SAN:
I've heard all about Thakin Soe. There's nothing new in that. There isn't a decent man among those Red-flags. They're all jail birds, thieves and desperadoes, who take cover under the Red flag racket. They're not really even rebels.

AYE NYEIN:
There are choice bits about Thakin Than Tun, too.

THA SAN *(taking his eyes away from the spot he is watching)* :
What does it say? But wait. Who is turning out these leaflets?

AYE NYEIN :
The secret H.Q. of the Peace Guerrillas, it says.

THA SAN *(interested)* :
Let me see. *(He takes the leaflet from Aye Nyein. While he is turning it over a couple of shots are heard in the distance. He at once hands the leaflet back to Aye Nyein and returns to his watch.)*

AYE NYEIN :
That's right, watch for those bastards. I'll read it out to you. *(Reading)* :

THAKIN THAN TUN OF BURMA.

Thakin Than Tun comes from a family of small land-owners. There's no one to touch him for shiftiness and sharp practice. He gave himself away even in the day of the Peacock magazine, when he was a beginner in politics, and he's been the same right up to now. He can never get over his goings-on when held office during the Japanese regime when he went gold-digging. In Moulmein and Pyapon and everywhere. He was quite shameless in helping himself to the Anti-Japanese Resistance funds. He made it seem that he was the only Minister who supported the Communist movement and wouldn't let any one else get into the act.

Look at the way he neglected his job and hid in a

corner during the Resistance. He came out only when
the Allies came in, and then began posing as one of the
top leaders. He's a head above everyone in treachery
to his comrades. He can give a lesson to everyone in
that kind of thing. Look at the way he told lies to the
British authorities as soon as the Resistance was successfully over, and betrayed his fellow leaders. Don't
you remember how the British Government treated
them? *(Finishes reading)*.

So much for Thakin Than Tun! These people seem
to know all about him.

THA SAN:

I did hear about that embezzlement when the split
between him and Thakin Soe started. As for the other
things this is the first I heard of them.

AYE NYEIN:

Just a minute I'll read you some more. Here they have
a dig at the Communists in general. *(Reading)*:

BURMA COMMUNISTS

1. During the struggle for Independence when the
whole people were united in a common cause against
the Imperialists the Communists tried all kinds of
underhand tricks to divide them, and when Independence had been won they got money from the Imperialists to stir up internal dissension and civil war at the
way they joined the tools of the Imperialists, the hillsmen, and turned to communal murderism under the
cloak of Communism.

2. They seem to take a delight in being a tool of the
risk of bringing the Imperialists back. Look at the
landlords and capitalists by provoking the daily

slaughtering of workers and peasants who are against landlordism and capitalism.

3. By their policy of destruction and murder they are reducing the whole people to poverty and the villages to ash-heaps.

4. Instead of the leaders teaching the people how to behave as good citizens they teach their followers to kill and steal, rape and rob, and to loot the public treasuries.

5. Instead of leading the way to social revolution they lead the way to civil war.

6. They call it a People's Revolution but they tie up with gangsters and recruit jailbirds who hold towns and villages in ransom. It's every man for himself trying to be the boss.

7. They say they aim at World Peace but in fact their insurrections and rebellions are destroying the chance of ever getting peace at home.

THA SAN:
Who is responsible for these leaflets from this Peace Guerrillas H.Q.?

AYE NYEIN:
I've no idea.

THA SAN:
I'm pretty certain the AFPFL is behind it all. These bastards don't say a word against Nga Nu and the AFPFL. It's the bloody AFPFL that does all the dirty work behind the scenes. Whatever did you keep this rotten leaflet for? Tear it up.

AYE NYEIN:
Only to show it to you.

THA SAN:
I don't want to see such filthy rubbish. Give it to me —
I'll tear it up. *(He takes the leaflet from Aye Nyein
and does so, scattering the pieces to the wind.)*

AYE NYEIN:
I get wild, too, when others slander our fellow insurgents. But it doesn't alter the fact that there are some
pretty dirty swine among us. I say, Tha San, I've been
wanting to tell you something. I couldn't decide for
some time whether I should or not. To be quite frank
I do not like the way Boh Aye Kyi is carrying on. Call
him a PVO leader! He is just a thief and a scoundrel.
Have you noticed how he always disappears whenever
we come up against the soldiers? He's going back to
the H.Q. for reinforcements, he says! He's running
back for more ammunition, he says! All bunk! He's
simply out to save his skin. But what makes me see
red is his getting away with party funds. I've caught
him at it twice. Do you remember what we got out of
that Muthiya Chattya? A whole boxful! I was there
when Boh Aye Kyi was emptying the box. There were
diamond rings, diamond earrings, diamond bangles,
gold bracelets, gold anklets and wads of currency
notes. But I was close by when he handed the stuff
over to the Party Command and he said there was
only one pair of diamond bangles and one diamond
ring, worth about 3,500 kyats*. What did he do with

---

* A kyat, or rupee, is worth 21 cents.

the rest of the stuff? Then again, when we raided that Chinese merchant's house we found, besides the other valuables, a good two hundred gold sovereigns inside the old couple's mattress. I saw it with my own eyes, but when Boh Aye Kyi handed the stuff in there was not a single sovereign there.

THA SAN:
Why didn't you report it to the Party?

AYE NYEIN:
If I did who would have the guts to take action against him? A hundred per cent gangster like him? And, look here, I know a thing or two about Boh Kywet, too. When we looted the treasury, we made quite a good haul. Well, he sent a lot of the cash secretly to his mother so she could set up an import license business in Rangoon. The others who *knew* about it said nothing because he gave them thirty or forty thousand rupees. These damned thieves have so much tucked away now that they are thinking of surrendering. But when we started the whole business it was *they* who clamored to fight against this dirty Nga Nu Government. *(Enter Ba toke with food packets)* Ah, food! I'm getting hungry, too. *(Ba Toke gives one packet to Aye Nyein and another, together with a folded letter, to Tha San.)*

BA TOKE:
Those bastards seem to be running short of ammunition. There wasn't much shooting last night.

AYE NYEIN:

Maybe. Hey, Tha San! *(Tha San has stood up suddenly gripping his rifle)* Hey! Where are you off to?

THA SAN *(going off in a towering rage)*:

To the village.

AYE NYEIN *(calling after him)*:

Wait, Tha San, Hey! Wait for the relief. *(Tha San goes off without looking back)*: What am I going to do if they rush me? What's come over him I wonder? *(To Ba Toke)* What was in the letter you brought?

BA TOKE:

I'd rather not say.

AYE NYEIN:

Come on, out with it.

BA TOKE:

About midnight the whole village was buzzing. That must be it.

AYE NYEIN:

Must be what?

BA TOKE:

Aye Kyi, of course. This Captain Aye Kyi.

AYE NYEIN:

What's he done now?

BA TOKE:

He was at Tha San's house last night talking to Mai Mya, Tha San's wife, until very late. Then he said he would sleep there and the silly woman made up a bed for him in the veranda. Just as she was going off to sleep, Aye Kyi came into her room and tried to get into bed with her. She shrieked blue murder, the whole village turned out to the rescue, and Aye Kyi slunk out of the back door. That's what Mai Mya has written to Tha San about.

AYE NYEIN:

Hell! I wish you had told me about it before you gave him the letter, Ba Toke. Old Tha San is such a head-strong fellow, I'm worried about what will happen.

BA TOKE:

Ah! I never thought of that! *(Two shots from the Government side.)*

AYE NYEIN:

I say, Ba Toke will you keep an eye on those bastards? I'm starving. I'll just have a bite. *(Ba Toke takes Aye Nyein's rifle and lies down in his place. Aye Nyein opens the food packet to eat. On opening it, he stares at the contents and then laughs.)* I say, Ba Toke, the packet of food you brought — do you know what's in it?

BA TOKE:
What?

AYE NYEIN:

Dog's dirt! *(Ba Toke, surprised, turns to look at the contents of the food packet. Aye Nyein slowly folds it up again.)* Well, well, well, poor fellows, they get the worst of it. Fed up with all this fighting! Of course they are! They are sick of the lot of us.

(Aye Nyein stares gloomily as the curtain falls.)

SCENE V

PLACE: *A country lane.*

TIME: *April, 1949. Enter a group of refugees carrying bundles and baskets in their hands, on their shoulders, on their heads. Some have children on their hips. The older children are being led by the hand. The old and infirm are being helped along. They all put down their bundles and stop for a rest. Some lie on the ground, others lean against their bundles.*

MAI SHWE, *a fat country woman (throwing down her bundle in a temper)*:
It's all the fault of this precious Government.

U PO MYA *(her husband, dumping his load)*:
Why blame the Government, Mai Shwe? Why not blame the real culprits?

MAI SHWE:
And why do you still stick up for your precious Government, when they've just burnt us out of hearth and home?

U PO MYA:
Look here! Don't go biting everyone's head off. You're not the only one who feels sore. I'm a bit irritable myself.

MAI SHWE:
If you're in a temper why pick on me? I'm cursing the Government not you. Why should you butt in?

U PO MYA:
Don't talk so wildly and hurt people's feelings.

MAI SHWE:
It doesn't hurt you. Mind your own business and let me say what I like about the Government.

U PO MYA:
Damn the woman! Can't you shut up?

MAI SHWE:
No, I can't! I can't! What are you going to do about it?

U THA DUN *(a Refugee)*:
Hey, you two over there, haven't we had enough to put up with already? Don't let us have any more, for goodness sake.

U PO MYA:
Well, speak to her. *She's* making the trouble.

(Mai Shwe scowls at her husband and goes on muttering to herself.)

ANOTHER REFUGEE:
Scrapping with your wife again, Po Mya?

U PO MYA:
It's not me, Tha Dun. She blamed the Government. I merely said, quite quietly, "Why pick on the Government instead of the real culprits?" and then she ups and says, "So you still stick up for your precious Government," she says. That's Mai Shwe all over!

U THA DUN:
Well, Mai Shwe, you do seem to be going for the wrong party. The Government forces didn't want to burn our village. They couldn't just stand by and do nothing when the Communists made it a stronghold. Where do you think the Communists planned all these ambushes against the soldiers around here? All from our village, so the Government couldn't help attacking it. And of course when you fight, you must fight to win. It isn't like a lovers' quarrel. The Communists took cover in our houses and therefore the Government forces had to burn them out with incendiary bullets.

U PO MYA:
Thank you, Tha Dun, for telling her that.

U THA DUN:
Ha! Ha! Did you think Mai Shwe had gone Communist?

U PO MYA:
God forbid!

U THA DUN:
You never know. It's a queer sort of time, this. You can't trust anybody or anything. You can't even talk freely.

(Enter Mya Gyi with four or five followers, armed to the teeth and badly needing a shave. The refugees gape at them in surprise.)

MYA GYI:
Hello, U Po Mya. What are you doing here? *(U Po Mya fails to recognize him and stares at him without a word)* I'm Mya Gyi. Don't you recognize me?

U PO MYA:
Ahhh! You gave me quite a scare, Mya Gyi.

U THA DUN:
You might have given us some warning, Mya Gyi. We're all jittery.

U PO MYA:
But what's been happening to you? You disappeared from the village ages ago.

MYA GYI:
Well, I couldn't go along with the Communists so I also had to go underground.

U PO MYA *(looking carefully to the right and left)*:
Was it true that the Communists captured you?

MYA GYI:
They nearly did but I gave them the slip and went underground.

U PO MYA:
Well, I'm very glad to see you again.

U THA DUN:
We all thought the Communists had tried you in their people's court and had you shot. That's why I'm so pleased to see you here with us like this.

U PO MYA:
And now, what are you doing, Mya Gyi?

MYA GYI:
I'm recruiting a company to fight the Communists.

U PO MYA:
And then?

MYA GYI *(making a gesture of shooting)*:
Fight them.

U PO MYA:
Have you got many recruits?

MYA GYI:
So far I've only got victims of the Communists and people whose relatives have been killed. I haven't yet managed to get any others. There are plenty who don't

like the Communists, but I can't get them to fight. But that's always our way. And some are just sitting on the fence. They'll hang out the Red Flag and be redder than the roses so long as they think the Reds are winning.

But as soon as the Communists run away, they hide the Red Flag, hoist the Union flag and welcome the soldiers. Miserable rats! But I'm still hopeful. One must do one's bit.

U PO MYA:
What about Government help?

MYA GYI:
Government help? The Government's got its work cut out to save itself, U Po Mya.

U PO MYA:
Not really?

MYA GYI:
It's just gasping for breath, and it's touch and go whether it survives.

U THA DUN:
Lord! Lord! That's a bad situation.

U PO MYA:
Tell us what you know about the way things are going. We haven't seen a paper or heard the radio for ages. We've been cut off from Rangoon so long.

MYA GYI:
On the Prome side the Army deserters have joined the Communists and are coming down the Prome Road with the White-Band PVOs and have reached Hmawbi. On the Pegu side the hillsmen from Toungoo have got within fifteen miles of Pegu.

U THA DUN:
Good lord!

MYA GYI:
In Insein, too, there is a hot fight with the hillsmen. The whole of Rangoon has the jumps.

U THA DUN:
Lord! Lord! Do you think the Government will pull through?

MYA GYI:
I don't think there's much hope. On top of it all the Government clerks have all gone on strike.

U THA DUN:
Oh dear! Oh dear!

MYA GYI:
In central Burma I hear the White-Band PVOs have taken over as the Government has been cut off. In Upper Burma, Sagaing, Shwebo and Monywa are practically the only towns left.

U THA DUN:
And what happens next, Mya Gyi?

MYA GYI:
Just what I said, the Government's at its last gasp.
*(U Tha Dun is silent. He stares at the ground. U Po
Mya is also lost in thought.)*

U PO MYA:
If this is the situation, is it worth while your trying
to go on fighting the Communists, eh, Mya Gyi?

MYA GYI:
Why not? It's got nothing to do with whether the
Government survives or not. I'm not fighting to prevent the Government from falling. All I want is to
prevent the people from being led about by a nose-
ring like castrated cattle; that's why I'm fighting the
Communists, Po Mya. I don't care whether the Government falls or not. I'll just go on fighting these
bloody bastards, and if the sons of bitches smash the
Government they'll damn well still have to go on fighting me.

U PO MYA:
That's the way. Stick to it. But you need a lot of guts
for a job like that. We Burmans don't care about anything until it actually touches us. So it's a pretty tough
job to wake us up. Still there's one thing; I don't know
whether it's just our luck, but the Communist devil
has shown his cloven hoof and now people are beginning to see him in his true colors. You may say I'm

talking nonsense but I sometimes think that this insurrection of theirs is really a lucky thing for the country. If the insurrection hadn't shown up the cloven hoof, they might have caught us napping and tied a rope to our nose before we saw the devil's horn and hoof. And the whole country would have gone under. Carry on the good work. Don't let us be turned from men into cattle, dressed by the Reds and led by the nose. Carry on and you'll be the savior of the whole country.

MYA GYI:
I shall be quite content if people come to realize how important my work is for their welfare. Whatever the difficulty, whatever the trouble, whatever the risk, I'd die ten times over. But if the people don't help no one can do anything.

U PO MYA:
That's true. But you know what people are. They see the bait but not the hook behind it. The Communists go round shouting their catch words: free land, fine houses, a little heaven below. And most people are just greedy fools ready to fall for anything. Hardly anyone stops to think what will happen afterwards.

MYA GYI:
We must do our best to get more people to see it.

U PO MYA:
That's right.

MYA GYI:
But, U Po Mya, I've been talking all this time and
you haven't yet told me what you people are doing
here with all these bundles and baskets.

U PO MYA:
Our village is gone! Burnt down! We picked up what
little we had left and started out, without even knowing where to go.

MYA GYI:
How did it all happen?

U PO MYA:
The Communists made our village their headquarters,
and of course the Government forces attacked it. So
the village has gone up in smoke.

U THA DUN:
As soon as they made it their headquarters I knew
it would go sooner or later. But I just kept it to myself and said nothing to anyone.

U PO MYA *(smiling)*:
You were the only one to think that. They were all
saying "Don't worry. We won't let an inch of the
village be taken."

U THA DUN *(smiling back)*:
They had to do something to buck us up.

MYA GYI:
Well, you two, I've got to get going. Goodbye. *(Turning to the other refugees)* Goodbye to all of you.

1ST REFUGEE *(coming forward)*:
Wait a bit, Ko Mya Gyi. I'll come along with you.

MYA GYI *(delightedly, putting his hands on Ohn Pe's shoulders)*:
I'm so glad, Ohn Pe. But you quite understand we don't get anything out of it? All right? Splendid! To have an educated man like you with us is a great help, a great help. *(Ohn Pe does not speak. He nods with a resolute expression on his face. They are about to go off when a woman refugee comes forward)*

AYE TIN:
I'm coming too, Ko Mya Gyi.

(They all look at Aye Tin)

2ND REFUGEE:
Who are you to say you're going? Is this the kind of job for you?

AYE TIN:
This is no time for parents to be telling their children who's to do what. If parents and children go on like this they'll all be changed into mere cattle. I couldn't stand that. Goodbye, Mother. *(She bows down before her mother)* Shall we be off, Ko Mya Gyi? *(They go*

off, Daw Pwa remains with her eyes fixed on her daughter)

U THA DUN:
There goes our first heroine!

U PO MYA:
Cheer up, Mi Pwa! It is a good road your daughter is taking.

(Daw Pwa, still looking after her daughter, makes no reply)

U THA DUN:
And where are the people who said, "We won't let you lose an inch of the village"?

U PO MYA:
So they did. And I know they meant it, too. You see the poor young Communists were relying on that Po Tun of Ohn Hne. The poor youngster didn't even know how to handle a rifle.

U THA DUN:
Who on earth is Po Tun of Ohn Hne?

U PO MYA:
Good Lord! Everyone knows Po Tun. Surely you must know him. The bandit Po Tun.

U THA DUN:
Oh, *that* fellow! The man who got a life sentence for

murder and plunder in Ohn Hne and made his escape
the other day. I know him, but didn't know he was the
man you meant. He's the kind of man who wouldn't
be afraid to tackle the soldiers.

U PO MYA:
That's what these young Communists thought. They
take anyone convicted of those crimes for a hero and
put great faith in him.

But gangsters are just gangsters and have only the
courage of gangsters. They're very brave against unarmed defenseless people; they are quite ready to attack them. But just let them catch sight of the police
and their pluck evaporates. So when the soldiers came
they made off hell-bent for leather. Ask Maung Taik.
He saw them. When the soldiers appeared Po Tun and
his gang were the first to bolt. Even the young Communists who hardly know how to load their rifles put
up a better show.

U THA DUN:
What a huge mistake it was for these young Communists to gang up with desperadoes and ex-convicts!
They're not the only ones to suffer. They've turned
the whole country upside down.

U PO MYA:
Of course. Just see what has happened. They dare not
face the soldiers but just run away, and because they're
afraid to fight, they hide in places where there aren't
any soldiers and break down the bridges, smash the

railway, set fire to the public buildings and burgle government warehouses. That's about all they can do.

U THA DUN:
They're not rebels — just rotters. They don't dare give battle, so they just give trouble instead.

U PO MYA:
It doesn't matter so much what they do, but it all has to come out of the people's pocket. It's the people who must pay for it.

U THA DUN:
It's beyond me. Couldn't they get power quite easily by getting the support of the people in an election instead of doing all this damage everywhere? Then the people wouldn't have to suffer.

U PO MYA:
I'm just an ordinary man and all I want is a quiet life.

U THA DUN:
Isn't your nephew, Nga San, Po Yin's son, one of the leaders? I believe he carries a lot of weight with them. Can't you get in touch with him and persuade him to follow the path to power through an election instead of causing so much trouble?

U PO MYA *(striking his breast)*:
I've talked myself hoarse time and time and time again.

U THA DUN:
No good?

U PO MYA:
He just preached back and tried to convert me. "Don't go along the opportunist road," he said. "Or you'll become an opportunist."

U THA DUN:
Huh! Whoever prefers the peaceful way is an "opportunist" to them.

U PO MYA:
Their views and ideas and ours are poles apart. Have you heard this for instance: "Religion is the opium of the people. Omniscience is all nonsense. Karl Marx is wiser than Gautama Buddha"? They go as far as that.

U THA DUN:
Who is this Marcus whom they consider wiser than our Lord Buddha? Not a Burman, I'm sure.

U PO MYA:
No, no, not Marcus. Marx, Karl Marx. I don't know what country he came from. After what Nga San said I didn't want to hear any more. So I didn't ask. But I did say to him, "A good thing your father died early!" I said, "If he had known that you were possessed by this Marx devil he wouldn't have died easy."

U THA DUN:
And what did he say to that?

U PO MYA:
He said that it was a great pity his father died without having heard Marx's doctrine. If he had, he would
have found his salvation. There! Enough to make his
father turn in his grave.

U THA DUN:
Lord! Lord! And what did he say about the Communist program?

U PO MYA:
What did he say! I was horrified when I heard it.

U THA DUN:
Oh! Tell me.

U PO MYA:
Why, there is to be a final World War in which Russia
will lead the Red Armies against the Anglo-Americans.
All the Communists in the whole world will rise up
against the Anglo-Americans on the side of Soviet
Russia. That is what they call the world revolution
and when that is successful the Communists will
create a millennium. That's the whole program in a
nut shell.

U THA DUN:
What's all this about a millennium?

U PO MYA:
The idea is that no one will be poor and everyone will be well off.

U THA DUN:
That's not a bad idea.

U PO MYA:
That's what he *says*. I for one don't care for the sort of millennium where you can't even listen to the radio program you like in peace, the sort of millennium in which you're frightened out of your wits all the time and continually spied on and can't even be sure that your own family won't tell tales about you and have you dragged off by the secret police at any moment; the sort of millennium in which if you let yourself go at all against the bosses you may be tried in the people's court and suddenly disappear. May the good Lord deliver us from a millennium like that; I don't want to see it, or hear of it, or think about it.

U THA DUN:
You can see that kind of a millennium all around us already. Just thinking about it gives me the shivers.

U PO MYA:
That's not the only thing. Once bitten, twice shy. There's a lot we can do for our people if we only stick together. And we've been had so many times I'm frightened of all these foreigners. If we must have dealings with foreigners in our own interests we should walk very warily. I don't at all relish the idea

of blindly getting help from any foreigners in creating
a millennium.

U THA DUN *(Smiling)* :
You're the Communist Nga San's uncle all right; you
talk far above my head. Let's have it a little plainer.

U PO MYA :
Didn't the British say in King Thibaw's time that they
would give us a better Burmese king and then they
too took the kingdom from us? That was once.

Then again the Japanese said we could join in their
East Asia Co-Prosperity and then they took over the
whole country. We have taken the bait twice, and if
we are foolish enough to take it again it will be entirely our own fault. I don't care a pice* for their
World Revolution. I don't care a pice for their Communist millennium. These catchwords leave me cold. We
must build our own future with our own people and
by our own efforts.

U THA DUN :
That's the spirit. Yes, politics is a tricky job. I don't
profess to understand it. Give me enough to eat and
enough to wear, let me go quietly to the pagoda and
monastery and say my prayers, and that's all I want.

U PO MYA :
These young Communists have got hold of quite the
wrong idea. If they hadn't started this insurrection

---
* Pice: Smallest unit of money.

and had quietly taken part in the election they might well have been in power by now. If not in the first election, they'd be sure to have won the next. Among the members of the AFPFL, and taking shelter under its cloak, some are ambitious, some misuse their authority, some seek their own ends, and some are dishonest, and people are quite fed up with them. So the Communists need only behave themselves and they'll have the whole country behind them. But as they are going on now they get blamed for the faults of the AFPFL.

U THA DUN:
That's a fact, Po Mya. Ah, well, times are getting worse and worse as we grow older —

(Enter five uniformed insurgents, all armed.)

INSURGENT LEADER:
Aren't you refugees from the Zibin Village? Where are you going?

U PO MYA:
Yes, we're from Zibin. Our village was burnt down in the fight between the Communists and the soldiers.

INSURGENT LEADER:
Zibin was always supposed to be pretty well-off. Now you are not so well-off, of course, but a thin elephant is still bigger than a buffalo as the saying goes. So I've got something to say and we insurgents always speak pretty bluntly. We need funds for our campaign. I

know you are refugees. What about us? We are fighting in the front line to create a new life for all you down-trodden people and to liberate you from the oppression of Nga Nu's traitor government. So we look to you to help us. I want to make it quite clear. You won't lose anything because we will make a list of all we get and as soon as we win you'll get full value for what we have taken. Come on now, hand over what you've got. Don't try to hide anything. Anybody caught at that sort of trick will be severely punished as a traitor to the Cause. Now, are U Po Mya and Daw Shwe here?

U PO MYA:
Yes, I'm Po Mya.

INSURGENT LEADER:
Come over to this side. *(Pointing to one corner)* Bring along all you've got. *(U Po Mya and Daw Shwe both cross over to the spot indicated, hugging their bundles.)* Is Daw Aye Mai here?

DAW AYE MAI:
Yes.

INSURGENT LEADER:
Come over here, too, with all your belongings. *(She joins U Po Mya and Daw Shwe)*

INSURGENT LEADER *(To his lieutenant)*:
Now, comrade, you search those people over there. Be careful to make a list of what you get out of them. I'll attend to the people here. *(The insurgent leader goes*

*to U Po Mya's corner and his lieutenant goes to the
rest of the refugees.)*

INSURGENT LEADER *(drawing out a note book and foun-
tain pen)* :
Now, U Po Mya, out with the stuff.

U PO MYA *(sighing)* :
Mai Shwe, give him everything and be done with it.
*(Daw Shwe, also sighing, produces from her inner
pocket all the valuables she possesses. The lieutenant
casts suspicious glances at the insurgent leader now
and again. The leader opens the parcel of valuables,
and pretends to be busily making a list of them. With
a quick movement he transfers some of the valuables
from the parcel to his trouser pocket. The lieutenant
see it, and grinds his teeth. The insurgent leader ties
up the parcel again and keeps it in his hand)*

INSURGENT LEADER *(pointing to the two big bundles
belonging to Daw Shwe and U Po Mya on the ground)* :
What's in there? Untie them please.

U PO MYA :
Why bother to untie them, my boy? Take the lot.

INSURGENT LEADER :
Now, Daw Aye Mai, we have been tipped off that you
have plenty of stuff with you. Come on, be generous
to us. To establish a new order for the masses is a
noble cause and deserves generous help. Mind you,
you'll get it all back; we are keeping an account of
everything we get. As soon as we have got rid of

Nga Nu's government you'll be fully repaid. So out with them.

(Daw Aye Mai also produces from her pocket her precious bundle of valuables. The insurgent leader unties it and goes through the pretense of making a careful list of the contents. Suddenly with a quick movement he transfers some of them to his trouser pocket. Again his lieutenant sees him and grinds his teeth. The insurgent leader crosses over to the rest of the refugees)

INSURGENT LEADER:
Now those of you who have not yet made your contributions come over here.

(Maung Htaik, U Sin and U Tha Dun come forward)

MAUNG HTAIK *(empting his pockets and offering a few notes and small change to the insurgent leader)*:
This is all I have.

INSURGENT LEADER:
What about that wrist watch? *(Maung Htaik stares at him in dismay)* Come on! Take it off. *(Maung Htaik slowly removes it and hands it over.)*

U SIN:
As for me, laddie, I am only a coolie living from hand to mouth. I've got nothing at all. *(Insurgent leader passes his hand over U Sin's pockets and lets him go.)*

U THA DUN *(unwinding his old turban from his head and giving it to the insurgent leader)*:
Here you are, Captain, take it, and don't bother to put it in the list.

INSURGENT LEADER *(waving him away impatiently)*:
Get away with your dirty rag!

(U Tha Dun retreats with a puzzled expression on his sly old face.)

INSURGENT LEADER *(to the refugees in general)*:
Thank you all. You've been very generous. Now you may go on with your journey. *(The refugees move off with what few little bundles and baskets they have left to them. U Po Mya and Daw Shwe are conspicuously empty-handed.)*

LIEUTENANT *(sternly, as he hands over to the leader his collection of the poor people's trinkets)*:
There is everything that I collected. But please search me, too. And you, too, show all that you got.

INSURGENT LEADER:
Of course, of course. *(Lifting the parcels in his hands)* Here they are, every bit of them. Come on, boys, let's have a look at the loot.

LIEUTENANT:
What about the things you put in your trouser pocket? We want to see them, too.

INSURGENT LEADER:

What are you talking about, man? Whose trouser pocket?

LIEUTENANT:

Yours! Yours! You've tried to cheat us of our share once too often. I'm not going to stand for it.

INSURGENT LEADER:

Who's talking about cheating? Be careful what you say, now.

LIEUTENANT:

Have you forgotten about the fifty thousand rupees which your wife walked off with hidden around her waist? Come on, come clean. Will you or won't you turn out your trouser pocket? *(He moves forward, whereupon the insurgent leader signals to one of his men who shoots the Lieutenant. As the Lieutenant drops, one of his own men fires a sten-gun at the insurgent leader and his follower. They both drop. The insurgent leader's remaining follower fires his rifle at the man with the sten, who fires back. Both are hit. All the insurgents lie dead. The sound of the firing has reached the refugees, and one of them, U Tha Dun, returns)*

U THA DUN *(surveying the corpses)*:

All dead! Poor boys! Poor boys! They talked a lot about revolution, but really they were all just dacoits. *(He picks up the pipe he had left behind and sighs.)*

(Curtain)

SCENE VI

PLACE: *A Village. A Communist People's Court.*

TIME: *August, 1949. The court is filled with on-lookers. The Communist jurors are seated in two rows. A batch of prisoners awaiting trial are squatting on the floor with Red police in charge of them. There is an expectant hush. Three Communist judges file in followed by an escort of Red soldiers. Everyone stands up and sits down again when the judges take their seats. The man sitting near the prisoners on trial, acting as court prosecutor, shuffles the papers in his hand and with a respectful bow places them in front of the middle judge.*

JUDGE *(referring to the first charge-sheet, calls out):*
U San Ke!

(The court prosecutor makes a sign, and U San Ke stands up. The judge takes a good look at him and then refers again to the sheet):

Father — U Kyu; occupation — trader; age — fifty-two. On June seventh, secretly listened to the Government broadcast. *(Looking up at the accused)* U San Ke, is it true, what I read out?

U SAN KE:
Yes, your honor.

JUDGE *(to the Communist jurors)*:
The accused admits the offence entered in the charge-sheet. Is he guilty or not guilty? If the verdict is guilty please raise your hands. *(All the jurors raise their hands.)* As the jury, representing the people, are unanimous in their verdict of "guilty," U San Ke; father — U Kyu; occupation — trader; age — fifty-two, is sentenced to two weeks' imprisonment and a fine of 2000 kyats. *(Turning to the jury)* If you approve please raise your hands. *(They all raise their hands. The court prosecutor makes a sign to U San Ke who sits down with a sigh.)*

JUDGE *(picking up the next sheet)*:
Ko Po Lone! *(Ko Po Lone stands up.)* Father — U Pyaung; occupation — cultivator; age thirty-six. On June fifteenth, at U Nyi Bu's house, you said to one U Kala, "There is no need to rebel against the Government just to get free land. The Government itself has passed the Land Nationalization Act to distribute the land; this insurrection is about as necessary as a comb for a bald man. The only result will be us peasants

getting it in the neck." Ko Po Lone, did you or did
you not say that?

KO PO LONE:
Yes, but —

JUDGE:
No buts. If you say "yes" that's enough.

KO PO LONE:
Yes, but —

JUDGE *(Getting angry)*:
No more of your "buts." *(The Prosecutor makes
frantic signals to Ko Po Lone to shut up. At the same
time a Red soldier standing near the judges raises his
rifle. Ko Po Lone does not open his mouth again, but
fixes disgruntled eyes on the judge.)*

JUDGE *(to the Jury)*:
If the accused is guilty, please raise your hands.
(They all raise their hands.) Ko Po Lone is a peasant.
Yet he does not believe in our revolution. He is a
peasant who believes in deviationism. He not only believes in it but tries to convert other peasants to his
heresy. If those deviationist ideas spread among the
peasants our glorious revolution itself will be in danger. Therefore the accused is sentenced to three years'
imprisonment with hard labor. Representatives please
raise your hands if you approve. *(All the jurors raise
their hands. U Po Lone sits down, very discontentedly.)*

JUDGE:

Thakin Tun Khin! *(who stands up)* Father — U Aung Ban; occupation — cultivator; age — twenty-seven. On June 10th, you abused our Red militia and told one U Bi "to put dogs' dirt in the food packets, not rice." Is that true?

THAKIN TUN KHIN:

Ever since the Red troops came to our village I've been among the people collecting food packets for them. Gradually the quality of the food got worse, and —

JUDGE *(interrupting)*:

Answer my question. Don't start a long rigamarole. Did you or did you not abuse the Red militia?

THAKIN TUN KHIN:

It wasn't what you read out just now. Please let me explain a little. Just a word or two.

JUDGE:

Hurry up, then.

THAKIN TUN KHIN:

When the food got worse, the Red Comrade, Ohn Khin, said to me, "The food is always rotten. You are no damn good." I replied, "Then get someone else who is damn good to collect your food." He slapped my face. I was so angry that I swore and said to U Bi, "These rotten Red troops are the bloody limit. But I never said a word about dogs' dirt, I'll take any oath on it.

JUDGE:
U Bi! Is U Bi here?

U BI *(standing up)*:
Yes, your honor.

JUDGE:
Is it true, what Tun Khin testified?

U BI:
True, your honor.

JUDGE *(to the court prosecutor)*:
Then why is it different on the charge-sheet?

PROSECUTOR *(to U Bi)*:
Why did you first come out with something quite different?

U BI:
You know very well, young man, I said exactly the same thing from the first.

PROSECUTOR:
No, no. You said something quite different then. You're telling lies now.

JUDGE:
How dare you tell lies in the people's court?

U BI:
I'm not telling lies, your honor. When he *(pointing to*

the prosecutor) first came and examined me I said the very same thing. But he told me to say also that Khakin Tun Khin said, "Put dogs' dirt in the food-packets, not rice." Then I said —

PROSECUTOR:
Hey, you old fool why are you talking such nonsense?

U BI:
We wouldn't dare to tell lies; we are much too frightened of you.

JUDGE *(to the Prosecutor)*:
Never mind, let him talk. I'll teach him a lesson. Just wait and see. *(Turning to U Bi)* Go on.

U BI *(thoroughly frightened)*:
I won't say another word if your honor does not want me to.

JUDGE:
Go on, go on —

U BI:
Then I begged him *(pointing to the prosecutor)* not to make me tell lies to hurt anyone. I even cited to him the old tale in which King Cetiya was swallowed up by the earth when he told lies, but still he kept it up.

JUDGE *(waving a signed statement a U Bi)*:
Then why did you sign this?

U BI *(pointing to the Prosecutor)* :
He made me sign it.

JUDGE:
Nonsense! Nobody can force you to sign anything.

U BI:
I was just a tool in his hands, your honor.

PROSECUTOR:
This old man is lying because the accused has bribed him.

U BI *(to the Prosecutor)* :
Young man, when we are in your power what we think about is not money, but how to save our skins. I realize that very well. You see now how much I'm afraid of you and how much I'm afraid of telling lies to hurt anyone. Besides, there's another point to consider. You say this Thakin Than Tun gave me money to tell lies. Where would he get the money? He goes around the village picking up crumbs, never has any regular meals but gets a scrap here and a scrap there. So —

JUDGE:
That's enough! *(To the Jury)* If Thakin Tun Khin is guilty raise your hands. *(They all raise their hands.)* The accused Tun Khin is not only guilty of ingratitude to the Red comrades who are laying down their lives to establish a new order for the people, but he has also instigated others to be disrespectful to the Red militia. Thirty stripes and three years. *(To the Jury)* If you

approve raise your hands. *(They all raise their hands.)*
U Bi, also for giving false evidence in favor of Thakin
Tun Khin one year. If you approve raise your hands.
(They all raise their hands.)

JUDGE:
Ba Zan! *(Ba Zan stands up)* Father — U Kya; occupation—cultivator; age—twenty-eight. On May 22nd,
you went to fetch the soldiers. Is that correct?

BA ZAN *(scowling and shortly)*:
No.

JUDGE:
What do you mean, no? You did! You traitors must
be wiped out. It was just because traitors like you
were not shot that the Paris Commune failed. You are
guilty. What have you to say?

BA ZAN:
I'm not.

JUDGE:
You are.

BA ZAN:
I'm not.

JUDGE *(hotly)*:
Yes! You are.

BA ZAN *(hotly)*:
No! I'm not.

RED SOLDIER *(aiming his rifle at Ba Zan)*:
Hey, you! Do you want your brains blown out?

BA ZAN *(bursting into tears with anger)*:
Kill me then, kill me. The sooner I'm dead the sooner
I shall get some peace.

RED SOLDIER:
Wise guy!

BA ZAN:
How could I have gone to fetch the soldiers when I've
never even set eyes on them? I wouldn't know them if
I saw them. But you won't believe me. You believe
whatever your spies tell you. They beat me, they cruci-
fied me, they twisted my . . .

JUDGE:
Shut up, you!

BA ZAN *(turning to the spectators)*:
These fellows are going to murder me —

JUDGE *(with a wave of his hand to the Red soldiers)*:
Take him away, take him away, and make an example
of him.

*(The Red soldiers drive Ba Zan out of the court with
kicks and blows which do not stop his shouting.*

BA ZAN:
These Communists are murdering me. I'm not guilty!

The brutes are murdering me! All I want is a fair trial by the people.

(The Judge indicates that the session is over. He stands up, but then, as if he has just remembered something, he sits down again, and turning to the jury)

JUDGE:
If Ba Zan is guilty raise your hands.
(All the jury members raise their hands. And while their hands are still raised the curtain falls.)

SCENE VII

PLACE: *A house in Nyaungbintha village.*

TIME: *January, 1950. Enter villagers in twos and threes. While the room is filling, rhythmic shouting of slogans off-stage by a large party coming to the house:*

> "Who tread upon the people?
>   *Our enemies!"*
> "Who treat them like cattle?
>   *Our enemies!"*
> "Down with dictators —
>   *Away with them."*
> "Political robbers —
>   *Away with them."*
> "Tread upon the people —
>   *Fire will blaze."*
> "Treat them as cattle —
>   *Fire will blaze."*
> "The people are rising —
>   *We win, we win!"*

*(Enter Mya Gyi followed by Ohn Pe, Tha Hla and Ba
Zan. Behind them the slogan-shouting villagers crowd
in. When they have taken up their various places there
is silence.)*

MYA GYI:

To put it plainly, we are not fighting because we have
clever ideas or wonderful aims, but because we just
can't stand this Communist tyranny any longer. If we
don't stand up for ourselves and make a fight of it,
we shall be like Mai Dwe in the story who was gradually swallowed by the dragon. The Communists will
have a ring in our nose and lead us about like cattle.
It will be too late then for us to kick against the jabs.
They will drive us just as they like and when we've
done with work they'll send us to the slaughter house.
These bas—, pardon me, these blighters fool us all the
time with their damned catch-words—the "millennium"—"the new order"—"the welfare world"—
and all the time it is *they* who live like lords. It is *their*
millennium. We don't see anything of it.

A MAN:

They've given us a "new order" already.

MYA GYI:

Yes?

MAN:

Talk out loud, and you are hauled off to the people's
court; break wind, and you are hauled off to people's
court; you can't even ease yourself, without being

hauled off to the people's court. Every now and then people find themselves crammend into cattle-pounds. Every now and then people disappear. What they say is quite true; for us it is a "new order" all right.

(General laughter)

MYA GYI *(smiling)* :
Well, folks, I've said what I know. Ohn Pe will speak next. Ohn Pe!

OHN PE:
What I've to say is quite short. From the point of view of the whole country, those who are fighting are of two kinds, those who want to get into power legally, and those who want to get in by force. These are the only two kinds, broadly speaking. Now which of them do you prefer? If you prefer those who want power by legal means, you vote for the candidates you like and not for the ones you don't like. You can tell them what you want them to do for you. You can also tell them what you don't like about what they are doing. If you don't like their work at all you don't vote for them again and turn them out.

As for those who take power by force, you'll have to accept them whether you like them or not. You won't be able to tell them what you want; you'll have to put up with what they happen to want. If you don't like what they do you won't be able to say so openly, and you won't be able to get rid of them. You'll be helpless as cattle led to slaughter. The people who want power by legal means are democrats. The men in the robber gang are Communists. If you prefer the Communists, even before you know where their promised land is, you will have to surrender to them all your freedom. Even now, what about your former freedom? Can you live in peace and security? Can you come and go where you like in safety? Can you even open your mouth without the fear of spies reporting against you? In any village under Communist control at least three-quarters of the villagers are their spies in one way or another. You hardly even dare get rid of a bit of wind. Now, Ko Ba Zan! *(Ko Ba Zan comes forward. Laying his hand on Ko Ba Zan's shoulder, Ohn Pe continues)* Here's someone who has been through it all. Our old friend Ba Zan will tell you all about it. He was sentenced to death by the Communist people's court. Luckily for him, Ko Mya Gyi and our guerrillas managed to rescue him. Listen to him.

BA ZAN :

The Communists turned loose many spies in our village. We were all in holy terror of these spies. One word from them, and off you went to the poeple's court. They accused me of going to fetch the soldiers. The people's court for me. Four days before my case came up they wanted me to make a confession. They tortured me to confess. Of course I couldn't confess to a crime I wasn't guilty of. So they carried me off into the jungle and there — my shins still ache from their blows — they hung me head-down from a tree and beat me to get my confession. They did a lot of things to me which I would rather not speak about. I was half dead when they finished with me. As for those they really hated, the poor devils were bayonetted to death in public. The whole village had to turn out to see "justice" done!

In their so-called prisons there was barely room even for one man to sit down. Just pig pens. There you were cooped up all day, except twice a day when you were led out to relieve yourself. That was your "exercise" too.

Even monks were not spared. They were forced to take off their yellow robes and join the recruits under training.

MYA GYI:

There! You've all heard with your own ears, and seen with your own eyes; and some of you have suffered yourselves. Are you going to hang back as if nothing matters until it touches you personally. It's Ba Zan today. Any one of you tomorrow. We are fighting now because we don't know when our turn will come, so we mean to get our blow in first. I'll be frank with you. We're in a tight corner and by no means out of the woods yet. For all I know the Communists might get us all tomorrow. But we don't mind whether we win or lose. But it will be a sad tale if we don't raise a finger to stop them. We'll simply be sticking out our necks. So that is why we are rising to try and smash them. And we want you and all true Burmans to join us.

But there is just one more point.

We want recruits. But we don't want opportunists and we don't want people who merely sit on the fence. You can't trust people like that. They'll join us and when they think the other side is winning they'll turn their coats. They are like monsters with two bottoms.

And we don't want brigands who are out for loot. I'll speak quite plainly. To go along with people like that is no better than going along with a viper inside your shirt. U Tha Byaw, are you with us?

U THA BYAW:
Sorry, I can't manage it, Mya Gyi. It's a shame but I have to think of my family.

MYA GYI:
Htwe Maung, what about you?

HTWE MAUNG:
Like a shot! I've a score to settle with the Communist swine who shot my brother.

MA MYA KHIN:
Me too, Ko Mya Gyi.

(Distant sound of rifle fire. Some of the people disappear. Mya Gyi's guerrillas grab their rifles and go out to fight.)

OHN PE:
(Picking up his rifle) Mya Gyi, you stay here a while. I'll go see what's up. *(Exit Ohn Pe. Rifle fire gets louder.)*

MYA GYI:
Keep your heads down. *(Mya Gyi's first female recruit — the heroine of Zibin village — Aye Tin, picks up a*

*rifle and is just about to go out when Ba Zan grabs
her rifle and goes off himself.)*

MYA GYI:
Now, you people, you'd better get away quickly. Don't
run. You might be shot by mistake. *(Exit villagers one
by one. When the last one has gone, Mya Gyi goes to
the door and encounters Ohn Pe who has been wounded
and is being helped into the room by Ba Zan and a
villager.)*

MYA GYI:
Hello, Ohn Pe! *(Seeing that Ohn Pe is severely
wounded, Mya Gyi takes him into his arms.)* Where
are you hit? How did it happen?

BA ZAN:
A blasted Communist sniper got him.

VILLAGER:
Lots of those bastards have already got into the village.

OHN PE:
Ko Mya Gyi, hurry up and get away. There are too
many of them.

MYA GYI:
Give me a hand here. I'll lift his head.

OHN PE:
Don't worry about me. I've had it. Save yourselves.

MYA GYI:

Rubbish! We'll take you with us. We'll die together if we must.

OHN PE:

Mya Gyi, you are the leader. Don't be so soft. You can't spoil the whole show just for me. Get out, all of you, but shoot me before you go. Don't leave me half dead in the hands of the Communists.

MYA GYI:

We couldn't do that! Come, we'll take you with us. *(While he is trying to lift up Ohne Pe, the sounds of rifle fire and the shouts of the Communists can be heard very close.)*

OHN PE:

Mya Gyi, the people trust us. We're certain to win through. You must carry on the good work. Please don't allow the Communists to catch you here like rates, just on my account. *(Raising his voice)* Aye Tin! Have you forgotten your promise? *(Aye Tin seems to have awakened from a stupor. She squares her jaw and drawing the revolver at her waist shoots Ohn Pe twice. Mya Gyi taken aback, is speechless. Then pulling himself together he gives a word of command and they all disappear amidst the din of shouts and gunfire.)*

SCENE VIII

PLACE: *Communist Party Divisional H.Q.*

TIME: *March, 1950. Aung Win is seated at a table studying some papers. Presently Chit Tun enters with a parcel in his hand.*

CHIT TUN:
Ko Aung Win, the messenger you sent home has returned. He has brought back this parcel and a letter for you. *(He gives them to Aung Win, who breaks into a smile of pleasure as he lays the parcel on the table and opens the letter.)*

AUNG WIN *(as he smilingly reads the letter)*:
Tet Toe is a smart lad. He can write quite well now.

CHIT TUN:
What does he say?

AUNG WIN:
Listen to this: *(reading aloud)*
Dear Daddy,

We have had your letter. Mummy is not well. So I am replying for her. It is two years now since you went away. Hla Hla often asks Mummy to call you home. Then you don't come and Hla Hla bursts into tears. Then Grandpa says to her, "There, there, little lady, your Dad is doing work for the country and the people, so don't cry!" Then Grandpa starts crying, and when Mummy sees that she cries. And Aunty cries. I cry, too, Daddy. We miss you very badly, Daddy. Please come home now.

Grandpa says that Daddy and Daddy's friends can find power in the circle of Democracy. I have drawn a circle for you on the next page.

If Daddy comes into the circle Daddy need not be separated from us anymore. Hla Hla won't cry for Daddy anymore. Mummy won't cry. Aunty won't cry. Come home, Daddy. Come and find power within the circle together with Sonny and all of us.

                                   Your loving
                                        Sonny Tet Toe

CHIT TUN:
How old is Tet Toe now?

AUNG WIN:
He must be ten now.

CHIT TUN:
Not a bad effort for a ten-year-old.

AUNG WIN:
He's very bright and very loving, too.

CHIT TUN:
Well, well. What time does today's meeting start?

AUNG WIN:
As soon as those fellows arrive.

CHIT TUN:
Do you think they will come? I rather doubt it.

AUNG WIN:
Their reply said quite definitely that they would attend.

CHIT TUN:
Do get things fixed up at this meeting.

AUNG WIN:
It's only because of Party orders that I'm holding it.
Personally I'm not very keen on joining up with this
crowd.

CHIT TUN:
What's the objection?

AUNG WIN:
Those chaps have no discipline. Anyone with a uni-
form can join them. Their organization is full of all
sorts of riff-raff, thieves, spies, brothel keepers and
brigands. To join up with a lot like that is silly. I'd
much rather rely on ourselves.

CHIT TUN:

I agree with you there. I don't know what you think, but for some time now, I've been losing faith in ourselves. *(Aung Win makes no reply. He looks down and nods.)* I don't like the way some of our fellows are carrying on. If I were to tell the Party the things I know, we should all start shooting each other. *(Aung Win, still gazing at the floor, sighs.)* The worst of them all is Boh Tauk Tun. He is getting above himself—practically lording it over us. I sometimes feel like shooting it out with him and taking my chance.

AUNG WIN *(getting up from his chair)*:

That's enough, my dear Chit Tun. What you know is nothing compared to what I know. I have to hold myself in, but I'm sure to break out some way.

CHIT TUN:

It's the same with me. The only question is when.

AUNG WIN *(sighing)*:

Oh, well, we must make the best of a bad job. We've gone the wrong way from the very beginning. It was a big mistake to rush into insurrection without proper preparation. Insurrection is not child's play. It is not a thing to be undertaken in the heat of the moment, or for idle vanity, or just because other people egg us on. It is not a thing to be done because of a few leaders who want an insurrection because they don't know any other way to show themselves important. I'm not ashamed to admit that I didn't understand at first.

Now I know. I realize it more and more every day.

It's not all the little mistakes we keep on finding out now. They're just the penalty for the first mistake we made in rushing headlong into insurrection. The truth is that if we had had made careful plans from the beginning no dacoits like Tauk Tun, lechers like Tin Maung, murderers like Po Thein, gangsters like Sein Tin, could have got in as leaders. If we had made careful plans from the beginning we would never have joined up with the outfit from the hills and the White Band PVOs.

Since we had made no careful plans we tried to run before we could walk and were never content to take one step at a time. We jumped at any chance and chucked our line in wherever we saw the waters bubbling. When we found we had made a mistake we made another mistake in trying to set it right. More mistakes, more corrections, more mistakes round and round all the time in a vicious circle. That's been our way, Chit Tun, hasn't it?

If we had made careful plans would we ever have joined up even for a moment with this collection of thieves, loafers and riff-raff, who call themselves the White Band PVOs? Would we have joined up even for a moment with those Kachin whose war-cry was "Kill the Burmans" and who have been killing, raping and looting Burmese villagers? Of course not! Because we had made no careful plans we never stopped to think that we had nothing to gain and everything to lose by joining up with them.

If you don't believe me, wait and see. Whatever arrangements we make with the White Band PVOs we will have to fight them some day. I tell you, man, we will have to fight them very soon. And I'll tell you another thing. Whatever they may shout today — that they're ready to lay down their lives for their country and people, and all that — they'll only fight against the Government so long as it is weak. As soon as the Government is strong they will lay down their arms and go over to the Government's side. If the Government becomes weak again, they will change their tune again. So long as they're with us we have a viper in our pocket; when they change over, the Government will have a viper in its pocket. You just mark my words, Chit Tun, and say whether I am right or wrong. We shall also have to fight the Kachin group. As soon as the people in their desperation rise up against those hillsmen, we shall have to break off our so-called alliance with them. Then we ourselves will have to fight them, too. There you are, then. That's what I prophesy. If you don't believe it, waint and see.

So, you see, we are like bad actors spoiling a good play. We were conceited enough to think that we could act our parts without rehearsal. Now we ruined the play by bad casting and bad acting. Ah, well, I haven't given up all hope. We must profit from the lessons we've learned.

(Enter Thakin Lun, Thakin Chit Tun, Thakin Sein Tint, Thakin Sami and other members of the Communist Executive Committee.)

TIN NYUNT:
Hello? Those fellows not here yet?

AUNG WIN:
They ought to be here any minute now.

TIN NYUNT:
I say, comrades, have you heard Thakin Nu's latest boast? They have succeeded ninty-five per cent in their fight for peace, he says. Ha-ha-ha!

CHIT TUN:
Well, he's got something to boast about. He has got back quite a lot of us fellows and quite a few towns from the hillsmen.

TIN NYUNT:
That's nothing much. That old fellow is just a windbag. It was none of his doing. You know the crow in the story who got its bottom stopped-up by a mud pellet? Well, when he was dying of constipation, a friend advised him to sit in the water, until the mud pellet dissolved.

That cured him. But the crow, instead of thanking his friend for his advice, boasted that it was all because he had a broad bottom. Those towns were recovered not because Nga Nu is so wonderful, but because we were so rotten.

CHIT TUN
In my opinion our biggest fault was our failure to win the people over to our side.

THAKIN SAMI:
Our second fault was the continual fighting among our own fellow insurgents.

TIN NYUNT:

Yes, yes. It's all because of our own mistakes that we find ourselves in this position. Not because of Nga Nu. He's a cunning old chap, you know. He nicknamed his opponents Mr. Zeros. Do you know why? Because he is a Mr. Zero himself.

THAKIN SAMI:

That's right! I should like to ask him, "You call others Mr. Zeros. How many numbers have you got in your own head, eh?"

AUNG WIN:

I don't know him very well, Tin Nyunt. You knew him well, didn't you?

TIN NYUNT:

Yes, quite. We were in the College boycott together. And we were together in the Dobama organization and all through the Japanese occupation. He was good enough at writing plays and that kind of thing, but he knew nothing about politics.

AUNG WIN:

But wasn't he the leader of the student's strike in 1936?

TIN NYUNT:

What about it? Anybody could be a leader in those days. All he had to do was to curse the British. Even Po Toke, the opium eater who lived behind our house, could have been a leader if he'd known his ABC's. When he got drunk he used to curse the English outside the Government House.

AUNG WIN:
Still he managed to get his present job.

TIN NYUNT:
That wasn't his own doing. After Bogyoke's death there was nobody else to put in his place. So it was thrust on Nga Nu.

AUNG WIN:
Oh — ah!

TIN NYUNT:
You can easily judge what he's fit for. Now that he has come to the head of affairs all that he can think of for the welfare of the people is to dope them with religion.

AUNG WIN:
But from all I hear he is at least honest.

TIN NYUNT:
Hm, Ko Aung Win! you've heard the proverb: "The only honest men are dead and buried." He may seem honest enough to people who don't know much about him. Don't you believe it. In this world every man has his price.
(Enter two White Band PVOs, one with a carbine and the other with a stengun slung on his shoulders. Chit Tun goes up to them to take their weapons away.)

CHIT TUN:
Let me take care of your guns for you. *(The two PVOs exchange glances.)*

SECOND PVO:
We will take care of them ourselves.

CHIT TUN:
Can't allow that. We look after them during the meeting. You'll get them back afterwards.

(The PVOs again look at each other.)

FIRST PVO:
We can't do that; we will look after them.

TIN NYUNT:
That's not it; it's only just for the time being. It is the regular custom at meetings to hand in one's arms.

SECOND PVO:
We don't know anything about these customs. Either we keep our arms or we go straight back.

AUNG WIN:
All right, all right, keep them for heaven's sake. Let them be, Chit Tun. Come along and sit down.

(The two PVOs sit down with an unfriendly look.)

AUNG WIN:
The other delegates will be here soon. You don't mind waiting?

(The PVOs nod in silence with the same set expressions on their faces.)

AUNG WIN *(after a few moments of embarrassing silence)*:
We hoped that Boh Nyunt Pe would come along, too. Isn't he with you? *(The PVOs merely exchange glances.)*

AUNG WIN:
Er—, well, never mind. May we have the pleasure of knowing your names?

(The First PVO extracts a letter from his pocket and hands it to Aung Win.)

AUNG WIN *(opening it and reading aloud)*:
The bearers, Boh Min Yaung and Boh Thoung Htut, have been appointed delegates to represent me at the meeting. Signed Boh Nyunt Pe.
　　Oh, I see. *(To the 1st PVO)* So you are Boh Min Yaung? *(The 1st PVO shakes his head and points to the other.)* Oh, I see, I see. Then you are Boh Thoung Htut. *(The 1st PVO nods his head.)*

BOH TAUK TUN *(entering)*:
Hasn't the meeting started yet? Come on, let's start.

AUNG WIN:
The purpose of this meeting, comrades, is to acquaint you with the directives which have arrived from our GHQ. I'll start by giving you the substance of these directives.

(One of the PVOs pulls out a notebook and starts making notes in it.)

1. Thakin Nu's Government is now sending agents into our Democratic People's Forces to work against us from inside. They come in mostly under the cloak of White Band and PVOs. Since they started coming in the PVOs also have started attacking the Communist Party as well as the People's Forces.

2. The PVOs, under Boh Po Kun, Boh Htein Win, Boh Tun Sein, and Socialist Mya Han, without any excuse, made attempts to sabotage our Central Burma Conference.

3. On March 12th, 1950, the PVOs issued directives not only to make armed attacks on our Democratic People's Forces, but also to take over the Administration and set up a rival army.

4. The PVOs have already agreed to hand back our liberated areas to Thakin Nu's Government and thus wreck our insurrection.

5. The PVOs are parleying with the Army Chiefs of the AFPFL to make a combined assault on our People's Forces.

Well, these are the five points. We are instructed by our GHQ to ask you whether you are aware of these facts or not, and if you are, whether you are going to persist in this treachery or repudiate your own supreme command and come into our People's Forces. That is the question. What is your answer?

(The first PVO glances at his companion.)

SECOND PVO:
We don't know what your GHQ is talking about. This is the first time we've heard of these five points, and so we can't give our answer on the spot. We can't answer until we have put the matter up to our Executive Committee.

AUNG WIN:
That's reasonable. Please give us your reply when your Executive Committee has decided.

BOH TAUK TUN:
And be quick about it. We're not going to wait. Are we friends or enemies? The sooner you let us know the better.

(The second PVO scowls at Boh Tauk Tun.)

BOH TAUK TUN *(Returning the scowl)*:
Hurry up with your reply. Understand?

SECOND PVO *(Hotly)*:
We'll reply when we like; not at your orders. *(His grip on his rifle tightens.)*

BOH TAUK TUN:
If you don't reply we attack.

SECOND PVO:
If you attack, we attack.

AUNG WIN:

Now, now, now, we haven't come to that stage yet. So, comrades, please take these five points to your Executive Committee and let us know what their decision is. It will help us if we know quickly, because we have to report back to our GHQ.

SECOND PVO:

Very well. Now that you have finished your part of the business, we have to begin our part of the business.

AUNG WIN:

Oh! What is that?

SECOND PVO:

Last Saturday your people attacked our post at Gwe-Gyo Village and captured not only PVO Thein Mg and PVO Shwe Aye, but also made off with four rifles, one carbine, three stens, fifty thousand rupees, and gold and diamond ornaments. We want them back and our PVOs released.

(Aung Win looks at Boh Tauk Tun in amazement.)

BOH TAUK TUN *(jumping up from his chair)*:

No! Never! Get to hell out of here. Those two were not PVOs but dacoits. We'll capture the rest of them, too.

SECOND PVO:

Now, now, fair's fair. I was speaking quite calmly.

BOH TAUK TUN:

If you want to talk calmly, go and do it somewhere else. It's no good here. And if you'd like to know, those two dacoits of yours have already been tried by the People's Court and shot. So there's no good talking. Get out!

SECOND PVO:

We know what to do about that!

(Both PVOs stride out in a rage. Boh Tauk Tun pulls out his revolver and takes a step towards them, but is restrained by Aung Win.)

BOH TAUK TUN:

Them and their damned talk! Why not do them all in and have done with it? Why the hell must we always be consulting and palavering with these fools? They'll never be any good. If we're going to fight them let's have it out now.

AUNG WIN:

Leave them alone, Boh Tauk Tun. There are some things I want to have out with you, and I want to do it now.

BOH TAUK TUN *(taken by surprise)*:

What's the matter with you now? My God, the amount of jawing you people do!

AUNG WIN:

You always act big and talk big whenever I try to pin

you down. You can't get away with it this time. *(Slowly)* Where—are—the—fifty—thousand rupees and the other things which the PVOs mentioned?

BOH TAUK TUN *(mocking)*:
Where—are—they? None of your business!

AUNG WIN:
It *is* my business.

BOH TAUK TUN:
Why is it your business? Do they belong to the man your mother ran away with?

CHIT TUN, AUNG WIN *(together)*:
Hey, now!

BOH TAUK TUN:
Hey, now, yourselves! You poke your noses into everything. What risk have you been taking? It's we who do the fighting and risk our lives.

TIN NYUNT:
Don't talk rubbish, Boh Tauk Tun.

BOH TAUK TUN *(very angry)*:
Don't you go butting in. I don't want to hear what you think. It's we who fight and risk our lives. You're all just bags of wind. Shut up, I won't listen.

(He makes for the door in a rage. But Aung Win is too

quick for him. He stands at the door barring Boh Tauk Tun's exit.)

AUNG WIN *(pointing his finger at Boh Tauk Tun's face)*:
That's how you always carry on. All brag and bluff. This time you're not going to get away with it.

BOH TAUK TUN *(angry and astonished at Aung Win)*:
Answer? *(Drawing his revolver)* Here's my answer! *(Shoots.) (Aung Win is hit but does not allow himself to fall. He glares at Boh Tauk Tun with utter contempt.)*

BOH TAUK TUN *(shoots again)*:
Now you're answered! *(Aung Win falls. Exit Boh Tauk Tun stepping over Aung Win's body. Everybody is petrified with horror until Chit Tun runs up to Aung Win and takes him in his arms. The others crowd around them.)*

AUNG WIN *(with failing voice)*:
I'm going, Chit Tun. Please let me dictate a reply to my boy. Get me pen and paper.

CHIT TUN:
Pen and paper, quick, somebody. *(Someone fetches them.)* Thanks. Yes, Aung Win.

AUNG WIN:
Sonny,

I received your letter this very day. And this very day I'm leaving you forever. I've been shot. Be good, son. Let my fate be a warning. Revolution is not child's play. Sonny boy . . . *(dies)*

CHIT TUN:
Aung Win! Aung Win! He's gone!

(He becomes silent. Tears run down his cheeks. The others bend towards the two central figures in silent grief.)

(Curtain Slowly Descends)

END

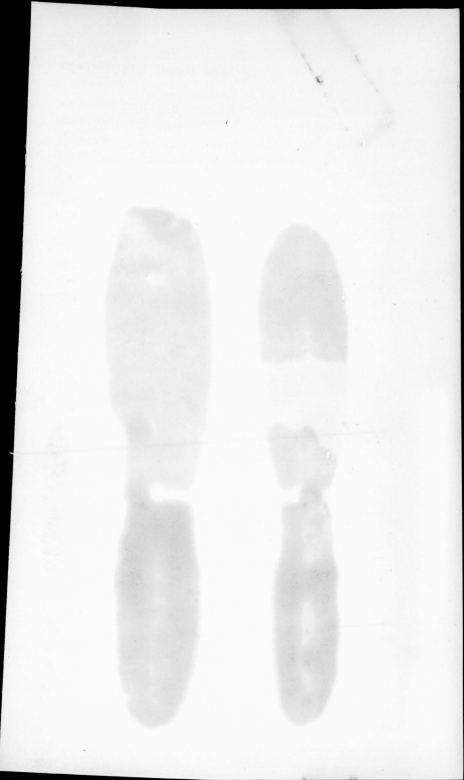